Contents

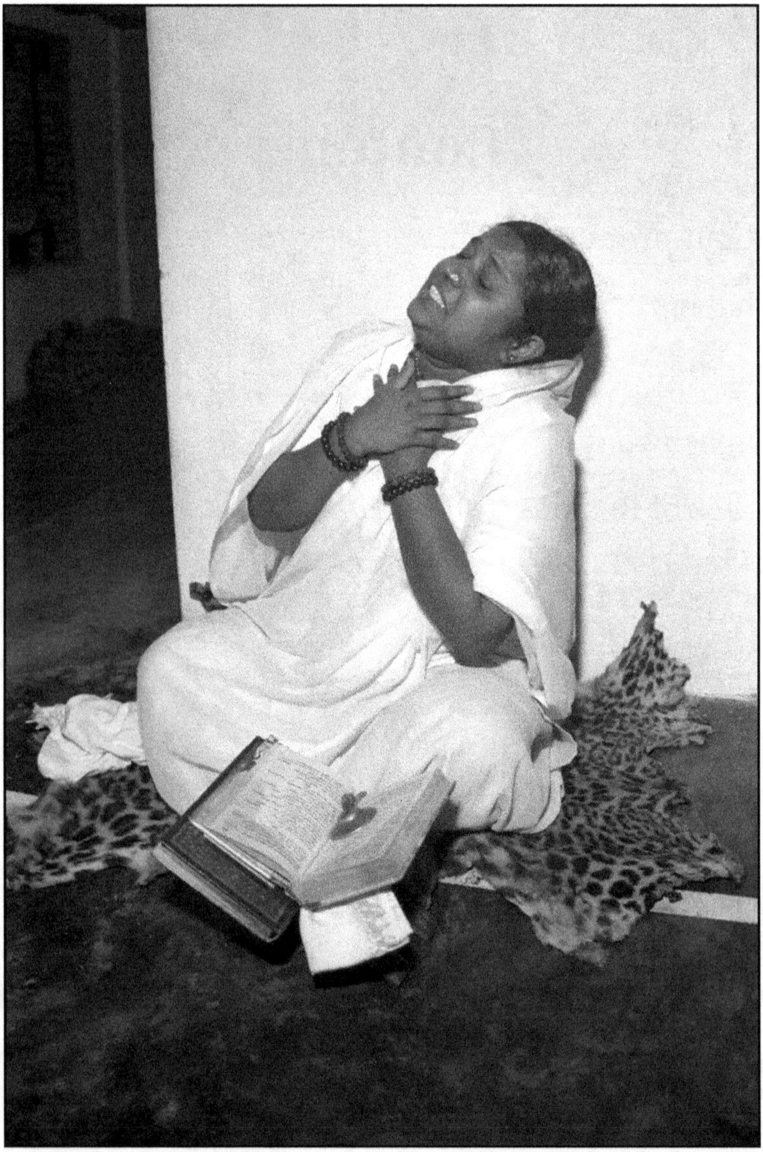

Bhajanamritam

Devotional songs of
Sri Mata Amritanandamayi

Volume 5

Mata Amritanandamayi Center
San Ramon, California, United States

Bhajanamritam
Volume 5

Published by:
Mata Amritanandamayi Center
P.O. Box 613
San Ramon, CA 94583-0613
USA

In India:
www.amritapuri.org
inform@amritapuri.org

In USA:
www.amma.org

In Europe:
www.amma-europe.org

About pronunciation

The following key is for the guidance of those who are unfamiliar with the transliteration codes of Indian languages which are used in this book.

A	-as	a	in America
AI	-as	ai	in aisle
AU	-as	ow	in how
E	-as	e	in they
I	-as	ea	in heat
O	-as	o	in or
U	-as	u	in suit
KH	-as	kh	in Eckhart
G	-as	g	in give
GH	-as	gh	in loghouse
PH	-as	ph	in shepherd
BH	-as	bh	in clubhouse
TH	-as	th	in lighthouse
DH	-as	dh	in redhead
C	-as	c	in cello
CH	-as	ch-h	in staunch-heart
JH	-as	dge	in hedgehog
Ñ	-as	ny	in canyon
Ś	-as	sh	in shine
Ṣ	-as	c	in efficient
Ṅ	-as	ng	in sing, (nasal sound)
V	-as	v	in valley, but closer to a "w"
ZH	-as	rh	in rhythm

Vowels which have a line on top of them are long vowels, they are pronounced like the vowels listed above but are held for twice the amount of time.

The letters with dots under them (ṭ, ṭh, ḍ, ḍh, ṇ, l, ṣ) are palatal consonants, they are pronounced with the tip of the tongue against the hard palate. Letters without such dots are dental consonants and are pronounced with the tongue against the base of the teeth.

Bhajans

ACHO MUÑCHĀ NANDALĀLĀ

Acho muñchā nandalālā (2x)
rādhā thī kōṭṭē tōkhē

Please come, O Nandalal. I, Your Radha, am calling out to You.

Tuñchē sivā mā jīnathī sagāṅg
sudh budh man jī buljī vanēthī
chānā hē rādhā śyām jī pyārī
hāṇē tū ach jēn murārī

Without You, my Lord, I cannot survive. I am often falling into unconsciousness. Am I not most dear to You, Krishna? Please come back, O Murari!

Tuñchī yād mē pigal jī vannāthī
śyām jī rādhā rōyē rōyē thī
dēr na kajēn ta giridhāri
dar kajēn dhukh asānjā

Constantly dwelling on thoughts of You my mind has begun to melt away. I am crying continuously for You. Please do not delay any further, O Lord. Please put an end to all of my sorrows.

ĀJĀ ĀJĀ RĒ

Ājā ājā rē kanāyī tērī yād āyī
ēsī anōkhī ghaṭā chāyī (2x)
ēsī mē kānhā tērī yād āyī

Please come before me, O Kanna! Memories of You fill my mind. The sky is filled with wonderful clouds that awaken in me the remembrance of You.

Sāvan tō āyō he man bhāvan na āyō he
ānanda dhām śyām man ānanda nā pāyō he
rādhē rādhē rādhē rādhē vraj jan sārē gāyō rē
vraj jan sārē gāyō rē

The rainy season has arrived and yet the enchanting Kanna, the abode of bliss, still has not come before me. My mind, therefore, has lost all happiness. All the people of Vraj sing, "Radhe, Radhe, Radhe!"

ALARNDA CHUṬARVIZHI

Alarnda chuṭarvizhi nōkkatināl
akhilattai āḷum tāyē nī
ammā entan āruyir ammā
lalitāmbā lalitāmbā

By the strength of Your eyes that sparkle with light, Mother, You rule the entire world. Mother, my darling Mother, Lalitamba.

Mahādēvanām śivanin mārbinai
malarttiruvaṭiyāl varuṭi nirkiṛāy
attiruppādam ennil patiyavē
tavikkiṛatamma en idayam
lalitāmbā lalitāmbā

With Your tiny feet, You stand on the chest of the supreme Lord Shiva. My heart aches with longing for the gentle touch of those blessed feet, O Lalitamba.

Mummūrttikaḷaiyum surāsurarkaḷaiyum
aṇṭa charācharam anaittaiyum untan
ni tirumalaraṭi chalankayāy aṇindu
āṭukiṛāy nī lalitāmbā lalitāmbā

The mighty gods, the venerable sages, all of creation itself, all that is alive or still, all of that do You tie onto Your anklets when You dance in bliss, Lalitamba.

Nilaiyillāta māyā ulakil
nin padamalarē entan tañcham
nin tirumalaraṭi śaraṇam śaraṇam
lalitāmbā lalitāmbā

Your sacred feet are the sole support of this fickle, ever changing universe. I seek refuge at those blessed feet, Lalitamba.

ĀLŌ MĪ MĀTĒ

Ālō mī mātē tujhyā charaṇī
jag jananī maṅgala kāriṇī
bhakti karū tujhī prēmānē
kṛpā aṣī hō mātā bhavānī

O divine Mother, the creatrix of the universe, we surrender ourselves at Your holy feet. Bestow upon us the grace to be able to sing Your glories with love.

Sakhā sambandhi tujhi āyī
tava prēmāchi tulnā nāhī
dukh manāchē dūr hōyī
darśan pāvūr tujhī śivānī

You are the only one whom I can call my very own. O Mother, there is no comparison to the love You shower upon us. All the sorrows in our hearts vanish the moment we receive Your divine darshan.

Karmāt tujhī pūjā karū dē
nām tujhē sada ōṭhī rāhū dē
sarvāt tulā bagūn āyī
sēvā jagāchī sadā gaḍū dē

May I worship You through each of my actions. May Your name always be on my lips. Seeing You in everybody, may I selflessly serve one and all.

AMAIDIYIN VAṬIVĒ

Amaidiyin vaṭivē anbin uruvē
amṛtānandamayī
alaigalē illā āzhkaṭal pōl
ānatun tāymaṭi

O embodiment of peace, personification of love, Mother of immortal bliss, Your lap is like the depths of the ocean which is undisturbed by any waves.

Chintaikal ellām kavarndizhuttu
śiva padattil nilaiyākkuvāy
āṇavam akattil talai tūkkum pōtu - nal
arivinai koṭuttu sīrākkuvāy
nilaiyillā ulakil nizhal pōl toṭarum
karmankaḷ tīrttu karai ēttruvāy

Drawing all of my thoughts towards You, please establish my mind in the state of supreme consciousness. When ego raises its ugly head within me, please correct me by blessing me with proper discrimination. The consequences of my actions follow me like a shadow through this fickle world. Please bring those consequences to an end; bring me safely to the shore of this ocean.

Inba tunbankaḷkkappāl ninṭru
iraivazhi atanai kāṭṭukiṛāy
anbum ādaravum illā uyirkku
aṛavaṇaittārutal tarukinṭrāy
dēvī nin tiruvaṭi sērnduviṭṭēn tiru
arulāl enaiyum ādarippāy

You show the way to the supreme state which transcends both joy and sorrow. Into the lives of those who have no love, You shower Your caresses and Your consolation. O Goddess, I have taken refuge at Your holy feet. Please show Your Grace to me; be pleased with me and show me kindness.

Anbin tiruvuruvē ammā amṛtānandamayī
anbarkkaṭaikalamē ammā amṛtānandamayī
amṛtānandamayī ammā amṛtānandamayī

O Mother of immortal bliss, You are the personification of love; You are the refuge of those who adore You.

AMBĒ JAGADAMBĒ

Ambē jagadambē ambē jagadambē
ambē jagadambē
ambē jagadambē ambē jagadambē
ambē jagadambē

jagadambē jagadambē jagadambē
jagadambē jagadambē jagadambē

O mother, mother of the universe, mother

Jaya jagadīśvarī ōmkārēśvarī
jaya hṛdayēśvarī mātē
jagadōdhāriṇi jaya bhavatāriṇi
janamana hāriṇi vandē
mērī vin ti sunlō mātē darśana dē dō mātē
mōhini tāpavimōchini tribhuvana
kāriṇi pālini mālini hē jagadambē

Victory to the goddess of the universe. Victory to the goddess of the divine sound Om. Victory to the goddess of the heart. Salutations to the Mother who uplifts the universe and carries us across the ocean of birth and death! Hear my prayer and grant me the vision of Your form, O mother. You remove all of our sorrows. O creator and protector of the three worlds, O mother of the universe!

kanmaṣa vāriṇi chinmaya rūpiṇi sanmatidāyini mātē
sakala surāsura vandita janani
himagiri nandini vandē
mērī vin ti sunlō mātē darśana dē dō mātē
mōhini tāpavimōchini tribhuvana
kārini pālini mālini hē jagadambē

O Mother, You remove our impurities. Your nature is the Supreme Consciousness; grant us good qualities! Salutations to You, O daughter of the Himalaya Mountain. O Mother, You are worshipped by the celestials and the demonic beings! ! Hear my prayer and grant me the vision of Your form, O mother. You remove all of our sorrows. O creator and protector of the three worlds, O mother of the universe!

AMBĒ MĀTĀ TŪ HĪ

Ambē mātā tū hī mērē jīvan kā dhruv tārā
tērē charaṇōm mē hī mā
mā pāvū sachā jīvan
tū mērā sab kuch he mā
mē tērī śaraṇa mē hū mā
tū mērī jīvan nayā jaldī pār karō dē mā

O Mother, You are the guiding star of my life. At Your divine feet I find true life. You are everything to me; in You I take refuge. Please hasten to ferry the boat of my life across the ocean of birth and death.

Tērā nām pukār pukār kē rōnēvālā hū mā
tū mērī dahan pukār sunē mā mērī pyārī mā
tū mujhē dē dē dilāsā
mā tērē milan kā pyāsā
tū mujhē jaldī darśan dēkē dūr karē mērī pīḍā

Mother, I will cry calling out Your name again and again. My darling Mother, please listen to my burning call. Please give me hope and consolation. I am thirsting for union with You; remove my sorrow by granting me the vision of You.

Pāp kaṭēmgē tāp miṭēmgē tū jab darśan dēgī
pāvūmgā mē jīvan kā phal is dam dēvī maiyā
tū karuṇā kar maiyā
mē hū nichāvar tujh pē
mērā jīvan tērī pūjā ban jāyē jagadambē

When You appear in front of me then all sins will be destroyed and sorrows will vanish. In that instant the goal of my life will be realized. Please be merciful, Mother, I offer myself to You. May my life become a worship to the Mother of the universe.

AMMĀ AMMĀ AMMĀ

Ammā ammā ammā
amṛtēśvari jagadīśvari amṛtānandamayī

Mother, Amritanandamayi, You are the goddess of immortality and the goddess of the universe.

Karuṇāmayī tū kṛpāmayī
dūr karō sab saṅkaṭ dēvī
karuṇāmayi kṛpāmayi amṛtānandamayī

You are compassionate and kind, O Devi, please remove all of my sorrows.

Jagadambikē laḷitambikē - tērā
rūp sadā rahē mēre man mē
jagadambikē laḷitambikē amṛtānandamayī

Mother of the universe, Lalitambike, let Your image be in my mind always.

AMMĀ BĀRAMMĀ

Ammā bārammā namma tāyi bārammā
guruguha jananī paraśivaramaṇi akhilāṇḍēśvariyē
akhilāṇḍēśvariyē ammā akhilāṇḍēśvariyē

O Mother, dearest Mother, please come before us. Empress of the universe, You are the mother of Muruga (Guru of Lord Shiva) and the wife of Shiva.

Parama pāvanē triśūla dhāriṇi chāmuṇḍēśvari nī
annava nīḍi poreyuva ammā annapūrṇṇēśvari
tri lōka jananī tri lōka pālini lōka rakṣaki nī
lōka rakṣaki nī ammā lōka rakṣaki nī

You are the embodiment of purity, O carrier of the trident. You are the Goddess Chamundi. O Goddess Annapurneshvari, by Your Grace we obtain our food and nourishment. You sustain and protect the three worlds. O Mother, You maintain this earth.

Śringēriyalli nagu naguttiruva śārada dēviyu nī
japa vannariyē tapa vannariyē ēnannu ariyē
ammā endu kūgidāga ōḍōḍi bārammā
ōḍōḍi bārammā ammā ōḍōḍi bārammā

You are Sarada Devi, the Goddess in Sringeri who blissfully smiles. I don't know anything about the repetition of sacred names; nor do I know anything about austerities. Despite that, when I call out, "Mother," please, quickly come running to me.

AMMĀ EN AZHAIKAYIL

Ammā en azhaikayil arukil varu tāyānāy
anpin mozhiyāl ennai tētri
tōlil sērkum parivānāy

When I call Your divine name, O Mother, You assume the form of a compassionate mother, and You affectionately come to this child with loving words and embraces to give consolation.

Piḷḷaikku tāyānāy piriyāta tuṇaiyānāy
anaivarkkum gatiyānāy aṭiyārkku nidhiyānāy
sīṭarkku guruvānāy sintaikku karuvānāy
kāṇkintra uruvānāy kāṇāta aruvānāy

You become the mother to this child and You do not desert me. You remain with me always. You are the sole refuge for all and the true wealth and prosperity for devotees. You are the Guru for Your disciple. You are the meaning for our thoughts. You are the visible form and also the unseen, formless consciousness.

Kaṇṇakku imaiyānāy karuttakku viruntānāy
kalaiyānāy kaviyānāy kada vulume nī ānāy
tozhuvōrkku arulānāy maṟai tēṭum porulānāy
paṇintōrkku aṟivānāy paragatiyum nīyānāy

You are the eyelid for the eyes and the subject that pervades every discussion. You are the embodiment of art. You are the poet, and You are the Goddess. For those who prostrate, You shower Your grace. You are the essence and meaning that all the Vedas search for. For those who have humility, You glow in them as the eternal knowledge. It is You whom all should struggle to attain.

Nānilamē nīyānāy nalla tamizh suvaiyānāy
telivāna manamānāy teviṭṭāta amutānāy
ulatānāy ilatānāy uṇmaipporul tānānāy
uyirukku uyirānāy ulakirkku varamānāy

You are the Goddess of the Earth and You are the taste of the sweet Tamil language. You are the clear mind, and You are that ambrosia that we cannot get enough of. You are the one that exists and the one that doesn't exist. You are the essence of all truth. You are the essence of life, and You are the boon to the whole world.

AMMĀ NĪ NĪḌU

Ammā nī nīḍu bā śakti manasige
jyōti nī nāgu bā bāla irulige

Mother, please come to me and strengthen my mind. Be the light in my dark life.

Ālisu ammana karayā nīnu
kandā ninnā muddāḍuve
nontā manake tampānerave
kandā ninnā muddāḍuve

My child, listen to Mother's call, "I shall pacify your sorrowful mind with the cool shower of My caresses."

Hagalā irulā kṣaṇa vellavū
haruṣa manadi mūḍalī
endendu ninna bālu belagi
kandā nīnu sukha vāgiru

"Let your mind be full of joy both day and night. May your life shine full of light. Be happy, my child."

Śānti jīvava tumbalī
prīti elleḍe haraḍalī
endendu amma jotegē iralu
kandā nīnu hāyāgiru

"May the eternal peace fill your soul and may love be present everywhere. Child, be at ease, Mother is always with you."

AMMA TAN MAṬIYIL

Amma tan maṭiyil kiṭattēṇam ennē nī
Tārāṭṭu pāṭi urakkiṭēṇam
Jñāna mām ammiñña pāl nukarnnīṭaṭṭē
Ānandābdhiyil āzhnniṭaṭṭē (2x)

Make me lie down in Your lap, Amma. Sing me to sleep with a lullaby. Let the milk of knowledge flow from You and allow me to become immersed in that bliss.

Amma tan kuññilam paitalallē ñān
Amma tan chārattu vanniṭēṇṭē
Kuññinu amuyāṇelyā mennōrkkanī
Amma tan mārōṭ chērttiṭaṇē (2x)

Am I not Your small and most adorable child, Amma? Shouldn't I come near You? Remember, Amma, You are everything to this child of Yours. You hug this child to Your chest.

Taḷarunnu manamiṭaṛunnu
smṛti maṛayunnu ammē
Vaḷarānāy vembumī kuññu paital
Aṇayānāy chārattu kāṇṇu nilppu
Ninnilēkkenne nī chērttiṭaṇē

I feel weak; my mind is wavering, and I am forgetting everything. This innocent child of Yours is burning to grow. Make me one with You!

AMMAYEKKĀṆĀNĀYINNU ÑĀN

Ammayekkāṇānāyinnu ñān vannapōl
akatārilpeytu ponnamṛta dhāra
ayiram ēzhakalāmaṭittaṭṭilāy
śaraṇāgatikkāy piṭañña nēram
dūre ninnu ñānoru nōkku kaṇṭā -
mandasmitattinte pālāzhiye
snēhappāl maṇam churattumāpālāzhiye

When I came to see You today, Mother, there was a shower of golden nectar within my heart. A thousand suffering children were seeking refuge in Your lap. I saw Your gentle smile that is as sweet as an ocean of milk. That smile is reminiscent of the sweet fragrance of love.

Peytozhiyāttoru prēmāriyō nī
tirayaṭaṅgāttoru snēhattin tīramō
arṛiyāte niṛayumā akṣayapātramāy
chiri tūki nilkkumakkārvarṇṇanō
paṛayumō ennenikkēkumā śāntitan
snēhattāl kōrttoru japamāla
nin tṛkkaikaḷāl tīrtta japamāla

Are You a rainfall that never abates? Are You the shore of the ocean of love? Upon that shore do the waves ever subside? Are You that dark complexioned Krishna who holds the wish fulfilling vessel that is always full? Tell me, will You bestow upon me today the rosary of peace that is threaded with love? That rosary is completed by Your divine hands.

Tinmayilēkku ñānariyāte pāyumbōḷ
arutennuṇṇī ennāru mozhiññu
munnilorāyiram vazhikal nīḷumbōl
muḷḷillā vazhi kāṭṭi nayichatārō

ahmenna bōdhamennullilāy pukayumbōḷ
keṭuttiyā putudīpam koḷuttiyārō

My Mother, the embodiment of peace for the whole world, is the shining inner Self of all beings. She restrains me as I run towards evil without realizing it. When a thousand paths lie before me it is my Mother who leads me along the way that is free of thorns. She extinguished the smoldering embers of my ego and lit Her own light in its place.

AMṚTAMAYI JAYA JANANĪ

Amṛtamayi jaya jananī tava tiru
kazhaliloraśrukaṇam ñān
palariloreliyavanivanil ninmizhi
patiyān kaniyaṇammē

O blissful Mother, I am a teardrop at Your holy feet. Please bestow a glance on this lowliest of mortals.

Karuṇālōlupa hṛdayam koṇḍoru
charitam nī menayunnu
acharitattiliṭam tēṭān pala
rakṣamarāy maruvunnu

With a heart full of beautiful compassion, You have become legendary. Many are those who have striven impatiently to secure such a place in history.

Surajanani tava padatār smaraṇayi
lozhiyum kaluṣatayellām
śataguṇavarddhitamākum pūrita
puṇyam pūmazha choriyum

O Mother of the Gods, all impurities are destroyed by the remembrance of Your feet; all of our virtues increase greatly, perfection is achieved and merits rain down like flowers.

Nirmala salila sarōvara hṛdayam
tanniloramibili bimbam
teli mayilaṅgane ninnu vilaṅgaṇam
ammē nin mukha bimbam

May my heart be like a lake of pure, clear water in which the moon is reflected. But in my heart let it be Your radiant face that shines clearly.

AMṚTAM TAVA NIJARŪPAM

Amṛtam tava nijarūpam jananī
hṛdayam tava karuṇārdram
sukhadam tava śubhanāmam varadē
charitam śivamabhirāmam

O Mother of enchanting and beautiful form, Your heart is full of compassion, Your holy name bestows happiness and Your story is auspicious and captivating.

Vadanam prasāda sadanam śubhadē
hasitam madhurasabharitam
alakam bhramarasamānam – lalitē
nayanam nalina viśālam

O bestower of auspiciousness, Your face is always clear and cheerful and Your smile as sweet as honey. O playful one, Your locks are as dark as honeybees and Your eyes as wide as lotus petals.

Vasanam pītadukūlam – vimalē
varadam tava padayugalam
gamanam marālamandam girijē
bhavanam natajana hṛdayam

O pure one, clothed in yellow garments, Your feet are capable of granting the wishes of devotees. O daughter of Himalaya (Parvati), Your movements are as gentle as that of swans, and You abide in the heart of Your devotees.

Jananam kalimala haraṇam jalajē
sadanam sudhāsamudram
naṭanam nayana manōjñam - mahitē
charaṇam bhava bhaya haraṇam

O daughter of the ocean (Lakshmi), You took birth to end the evils of Kaliyuga. Your abode is the ocean of nectar. Your dance is captivating and Your holy feet dispel the fear of samsara.

AMṚTAPURĒŚVARI MĀTĒ

Amṛtapurēśvari mate
akhilāṇḍhēśvari tāyē
jana mana mōhini māyē jananī
tiruvaṭi śaraṇam śyāmē

O Mother, Goddess of Amritapuri, You are the empress of the entire world. Mother Maya, You enchant the minds of all. I seek refuge at Your feet, dark-complexioned one.

Janimṛti śamanē śivadē
bhavabhaya haraṇē lalitē
śivamana nilayē śubhadē jananī
sumasama vadanē sukhadē

Source of auspiciousness, You who end the cycle of birth and death, playful one, destroying the evil of transmigration, O Mother, You reign over the mind of Shiva. Your face is beautiful like a spring flower and You grant solace to all.

Kuvalaya nayanē kamalē
kisalaya charaṇē girijē
kalimala śamanē mahitē jananī
kavijana rasikē lasitē

O Kamala, Your eyes resemble a lotus. Daughter of the mountains, Your feet are like tender leaves. O great Mother, You remove the evils of the Kali Yuga. Gentle Dancer, it is You who inspire the hearts of poets.

Śubhaśata nilayē nikhilē
paśupati dayitē sadayē
śivamaya charitē varadē jananī
vidhiśiva vinutē vanajē

Omnipresent one, the abode of all auspiciousness, wife of Shiva, You are the one who grants boons. The chronicles of Your divine plays are auspicious, O Vanaja, You are worshipped by Brahma and Shiva.

ĀNANDAMĒ AMṚTĀNANDINI

Ānandamē amṛtānandini – pūrṇa
āmōdamām svargganga nī
paramānandamē amṛtānandini
sāndramāy ni en svāntamākū

O Mother, established in eternal bliss, You are a heavenly abode of bliss. O supreme bliss, come and reside in my heart!

Mōhabhāvanatan varṇṇa rājikalāl
pāril viṇitalayum
papa bhāramām bāṇaśayaye
pulkiṭunnu manujan
lōkālāsyamitilē pōriṭaṅgaḷatilāy

dēhabōdhamām bādhayālulari
mṛtyu pulkiṭunnu

Man is deluded by colorful dreams of desire that lead to his fall. He clings to the bed of arrows formed by his sinful actions. Tormented by his identification with his body, he finally embraces death.

Prēma vāṭikayil snēha
mālikayil nalvasantamākū
jīvavīṇayitil prāṇā vēṇu
vitil dēvarāgamākū
yōgavīthiyitilē dīpanālamāy nī
jñāna sāramāy ēkabhāvamāy
mānasattiluṇarū

O Mother, come as the spring in the garden of love! Awake as a divine song in the veena of my life, in the flute of my vital breath. Awake as a flame of light in the path of yoga. Awake in my mind as the essence of wisdom, as equal vision.

ANBIN VAṬIVAM AMMĀ

Anbin vaṭivam ammā – tiru
varulin iruppiṭam ammā
vārīm vārīrē jagattīrē vārīrē

Mother is the embodiment of love and the abode of Grace. Come to Mother, everyone, please come.

Ullattai kollaikoṇṭa umaiyavalē
pāṭippukazhttiṭam murai ariyēn
vāṭittuṭikkum inda kuzhaindakalkku
nīnkāta nalam tarum iniyavaḷē

O Goddess Uma, You capture our hearts. I don't know how to praise You with songs. You are like the sweet mother who always bestows on her weary children what is good for them.

Vāzhkaiyin verumai akanṭratammā
āzhnda nal amaidi niraindatammā
chēvaṭi chīttattil padindatammā – atai
eṇṇiṭa kaṇkaḷ panittatammā

Mother, my life is no longer empty. I am filled with a deep peace. Knowing that Your holy feet are deeply imprinted in my heart brings tears of joy to my eyes.

Mūvulakālum ammā
mūvar pōtriṭum ammā
mutrum uṇarntavaḷl ammā
mutalum muṭivum ammā

O Mother of the three worlds, worshipped by Brahma, Vishnu and Shiva, the past, present and future are all known to You. You are the beginning and the end.

ANBUMIGU CHINTAIKALĀL

Anbumigu chintaikalāl mālaitoṭuttēn
sentil vaḷar kandanukku tūtu viṭuttēn
antamigu guhan neñchil iṭam piṭittēn – anta
āṛumukhan pērazhakai paṭam piṭittēn

I made a garland with love-filled thoughts and sent word to Kandhan (lord Muruga). I found a place in Guhan's heart and took a deep look at Arumukhan's beauty.

Vaṇṇamayil mītinilē vēlmurukan
val vinaikaḷ tīrttiṭavē varukindrān
tennakatte āḷukindra śilai azhakan
ennakattil kāṭchi tantān kalai azhakan

Velmurugan on the beautiful peacock comes to free us from bad deeds. The beautiful one who rules the south, the artistic one, gave me a vision.

Taṅgaratham mella mella asaintu vara
vaḷḷi daivānaiyuṭan mālmarukan
kaṇkavarum kōlattilē goluvirukka
nān vaṇaṅkum tiruvaṭivam kāṇukiṛēn

The golden chariot came swinging slowly. Inside of it were Malmurugan, Valli and Daivanai (wives of lord Muruga). This is an eye catching scene, the holy sight of the one whom I worship.

Orāṛu mukham kandēn uḷḷam makizhntēn
īrāṛu vizhi kandēn ennai maṛantēn
śīrālan uru kandēn śeyalizhantēn
chentāmarai pādattil śaraṇaṭaintēn

When I saw the six faces of my deity, my heart became overwhelmed. Seeing his twelve eyes I forgot myself. When His perfect form became clear in my mind I lay still and motionless and I surrendered myself at His blessed feet.

ANDELA RAVALI

Kalabhasundara gamanā kastūri śōbhitānanā
nalinadalāyata nayanā mṛdu manda hāsa vadanā
nīkai vēchi unnānu raghunandana rāvēlā

O Lord endowed with a beautiful body, Your face is made beautiful by the vermillion mark. Your eyes resemble lotus petals and Your lips form a soft and gentle smile. I am waiting for You, Raghunandana, why have You not come before me?

Andela ravali aḍugula savaḍi
raghakulatilakā nīvēnā
pakṣula kila kila prakṛti nṛttyamu
rāmā nīvu vachāvā
ambaramaṇḍē hṛdayānandamu
rāma smakṣamu valla kada
parama yōgulu chūṭa tapiñche
sundara rūpamu chūpavā

I hear the jingling of anklets and the sound of someone's steps as they walk. Is that You, Raghukula Thilaka? The birds are chirping and all of nature is dancing. Is it because You have come? So great is the bliss that I feel that it touches the sky. Is that because of Your presence? Please reveal Your beautiful form that even the Yogis long to see.

Vinna pamu vinavaya bankāru rāmā
vēgamukha nā mundu rāvayā
pannīti gandhamu pūsēdanu kastūri
tilakamu diddēdanu
muttyālakuṇḍala leṭṭēdanu
mallēlamālanu vēsēdanu
bankāru muvalu kaṭṭēdanu
kāñchana mukuṭamu peṭṭēdanu
nīku karppūrahārati nichēdanu (2x)

Please listen to my plea and quickly appear before me. If You come to me I will apply sandalwood paste and kasturi tilak on Your forehead. I will decorate You with pearl earrings, a jasmine flower garland, golden anklets and a golden crown. Then I will wave camphor before You.

Dōbūchu lāḍaku nā manasu
viruvaku īpēdarālipai dayalēdā
śrī rāma jaya rām jaya jaya
rāmā rāmā rāmā rā rā rāmā
nā māṭṭa vinavayya bankāru
rāmaya okasāri kanipiñchi muripiñchavā
śrī rām jaya rām jaya jaya
rāmā rāmā rāmā rā rā rāmā

Don't play hide and seek with me; don't hurt me anymore. Do You have any pity to spare for this poor creature? Victory to Rama. Please come before me, Rama. Listen to my request and show Yourself to me at least once. Grant me that happiness.

Jagadēka vīrā sītābhirāmā
rāmā rāmā rā rā rāmā
āditya kulajāta lōkābhirāmā
rāmā rāmā rā rā rāmā
āñjanēya priya hṛdayābhirāmā
rāmā rāmā rā rā rāmā
kaivalya dāyaka ātmābhirāmā
rāmā rāmā rā rā rāmā

O Lord, Your bravery is foremost in the world; You shine in the heart of Sita. Born in the Solar dynasty, You are the enchanter of the world. You are dear to Hanuman and You captivate our hearts. You Grant eternity to Your supplicants, O Lord. In You shines the Self unimpeded. Please come before me, O Rama.

ANKH NA PALKA

Ankh na palka rāma mādi
jagatanu bharaṇa karanāri
māri vālī ēk tu mādi
lalitāmbā lalitāmbā

By the strength of Your eyes that sparkle with light, Mother, You rule the world. Mother, my darling Mother, Lalitamba.

Paramēśvaranī chātiye dharī
nānu ēvu tāru charaṇum
tārā charaṇonā sparśana karavā
ātura ēvu mārū hṛdayū

With Your tiny feet, You stand on the chest of the supreme Lord Shiva. My heart aches with longing for the gentle touch of those blessed feet, O Lalitamba.

Dēvāṭi dēvō ṛṣi muni yōne
sṛṣṭinā nana charā chara saghalā
tāri pāyalanī sāre bandhī
nṛtya karantī tu lalitāmbā

The mighty gods, the venerable sages, all of creation itself, all that is alive or still, all of that do You tie onto Your anklets when You dance in bliss, Lalitamba.

Chañchala āsthira ā jagamāhi
tārā charaṇōnō ēk ādhār
tāri śaraṇē āvyā māṭi
lalitāmbā lalitāmbā

Your sacred feet are the sole support of this fickle, ever changing universe. I seek refuge at those blessed feet, Lalitamba.

ANNAI ENṬRATUMĒ

Annai enṭratumē en neñchil
ārvam perukudammā en
chinnañchiṟum vizhikaḷ unnai
tēṭi tiriyudammā

My heart overflows with eagerness when the word "Amma" is uttered. My tiny eyes wander in search of Thee, O Amma.

Udaya mukham kāṇa en manam
unmattam koḷḷutammā jñāna
katir vizhikkaṭalil āṭa
kattatru tuḷḷutammā

My heart is overflowing with the desire to see Thy radiant face. Your enlightened, glowing eyes should be the inspiration of my joyful dance.

Māykai viḷayāṭṭil en neñcam
mūzhki kiṭakkayilē un
tūyakuṟal ezhuntē ennai
toṭṭizhuttiṭṭatammā

While my mind drowns in the play of the illusion of this world, Your pure voice awakens me and pulls me away.

Īntravalē veṛuttāl sēyukku
ētu gati puviyil jagam
īntra dayāpariyē ēzhaikku
iranki arulvāy ammā

If the one who bore me despises me, what is my fate in this earth? O Mother who gave birth to this universe, kindly show mercy and grant me Your grace.

ANNAI KAYIL PILLAIYENA

Annai kayil pillaiyena amaidi koḷkirēn
anbu neñchil sāyndu sāyndu ennai marakkiren
kannil nīr peruka peruka kattu nirkiren
kalam thazhthamal karmam thīramma

Thinking of myself as a child in Mother's hand I feel peaceful. I forgot myself completely by resting in Mother's loving embrace. I wait with tears brimming in my eyes for You to please exhaust my karmas without any more delay.

Kaṇkal tannai imaikaḷ kūṭa kākka maṛakalām
kaṇṭru kūṭa pasuvai muṭṭi mōti pārkkalām
anai pillai uravu kūṭa ādhāyam tēṭalām
amma un tuṇayāle akhilam vellalām

One's eyelids may forget to protect one's eyes. Even the calf may poke and push away the mother cow. The relationship between a mother and child may become profit-oriented. But Mother, if one has Your divine help one may win this whole world.

Kūṭṭi kazhittu anpu kāṭṭum manita vāzhkayil
kūṭa irunda kāval koḷḷum daivam nīyantrō
aṭṭi vaikum kayiṛu untan anpu karankaḷilē
aṛinta pinnum tuyaram ēnō enkaḷ manankaḷilē

Mother, You are the Supreme Being who stays with us in this world where even love can be manipulated. The leash of our life is in Your loving hands. Once we know this truth, why should there be sorrow in our hearts?

ANUTĀPA SANGĪTA

Anutāpa sangīta svaravēdiyil
etra tālaṅgaḷum śōkarāgaṅgaḷum
īṇaṅgaḷum maunabhāvaṅgalum vividha
bhēdaṅgaḷuṇṭentu varṇṇōtsavam

In the music of remorse, how many rhythms, sad melodies, tunes, gaps of silence and variations there are.

Ārōhaṇattinte ātmāviluṇ-
tente dīnārdra mānasa rāgam
avarōhaṇattilō nirayunnaten
chittamaliyunna svararāga sudhayum

In the ascending notes of the musical scale is the music of my grief-stricken heart. The descending notes melt my heart with the ambrosia of their sweet melodies.

Etra tālam piṭichetra kālam kazhi-
chetra nāliṅgane nīḷum
viśrāntiyillātta sammiśratāḷatti-
lāṭikkuzhaññante jīvan

How long will my soul have to bide time, keeping rhythm and dancing with unsteady steps to this mixed rhythm?

Ālāpanattinnumārādhanattinnu-
mēkātma tālattinoppam virāgitābhāvattinoppam
tālam chavuṭṭi paṭhikkuvānammē nī-
yēkaṇē prēmārdrabhāvam

We will sing and worship You together, Mother. We will dance to a rhythmic song. Grant me dispassion for the world and devotion to You.

ĀYĒ HĒ MĀ

Dayā rūpē dayā dr̥ṣṭē
dayārdrē duḥkha mōchinī
sarvāpattārikē durgē
jagaddhātrī namōstutē

You are the embodiment of mercy. Your glance showers mercy. Your bosom is soft with mercy and You are the dispeller of misery. You save all from harm and yet You remain hard to approach. O protectress of the universe, salutations to You.

Āyē hē mā tērē dvār
darśan dē mā darśan dē
tērē prēm sē mā jhōli bhar dē
bhar dē mā jhōli bhar dē

O Mother, I am standing at Your door step, won't You give me Your darshan? Won't You fill up my heart with Your divine love?

Jab bhi rōkē bulāyā tujhē
bahalāyā jag kē khilōnō sē
na mānū mē mā ab kī bār
dēnā hōgā daras tujhē
dēnā hōgā daras tujhē

When I cried for You, then You distracted me with toys and the amusements of the world. This time, this child will not stop crying until You come. I need my Mother alone.

Āyē he mā tērē dvār khade mā

O Mother, I am standing at Your doorstep.

Arpit he mērē gīt mā
hē yē mēre dil kī pukār
na lōṭūngā tujhē dēkhē bin
khōl dē mā darśan dvār
khōl dē mā darśan dvār

I offer this song as the yearning of my heart at Your lotus feet. I will not leave Your doorstep until You open the doors and give me Your darshan.

Śakti dē mā bhakti dē prēm dē viśvās dē

O Mother, give me strength, devotion, love and faith.

ĀYĒNGĒ MĒRĒ

Āyēngē mērē kānhā āj
miṭṭ jāyēgi nayanō kī pyās
murjhāyē is jīvan mē
āyēgī ab phir sē bahār

My Kanna (Krishna) will come today. The thirst of my eyes will be quenched and spring will come again to this withered life of mine.

Āñchal sē vō lag jāyēgā
kah tē huvē mā, ō mā
pūchūmgī us sē rō tē hastē
yād kēsē mērī āyī āj
kanhā (3x)

He will hang on to the hem of my dress and call out, "Ma, Ma!" Crying and laughing, I will ask him, "How did You remember me today?"

Vādā usē karnā hōgā
chōṭ na jāyēgā mā kō kabhī
hōkē judā nandalālā sē
rah na sa kumgī ik pal bhī
kanhā (3x)

He will have to promise that he will never again forsake His mother. I will not be able to live even for an instant if I am separated again from my Nandalal.

ĀYIRAM DĪPAṄGAL

Āyiram dīpaṅgal ārati uzhiyum
avanītan avatāram mātṛatvamē
nilakkyātta alivindē alakaṭalē
nī allayō ammē satyamām satguru

To the incarnation of the Divine Mother we offer arati with a thousand lamps. Mother, the ocean of infinite compassion, aren't You the true sat guru?

Jīvita jvālā tāpattil urugīṭum
jīvanilēkku nī paninīru tūkavē
aliyunnu ammē nin snēhattil āyiram
aśarannar āyīṭum aruma makkaḷ

You shower the cool water of love on the souls that are melting in the heat of life's flames. Thousands of Your children, who are without any other refuge, dissolve in that love.

Māyā prapañchattil mōhāndakkārattil
mānasam uzharumbōl ulkkāmbu tēngumbōḷ
karaḷil kanivin himakaṇa māripōl
karayallē muttē ninakku ñān illē

Our minds wander in the darkness of illusion in this unreal world. Our hearts cry out and Your sweet words come as the soothing rain of compassion, "Don't cry my darling, am I not here for you?"

Tōrātta kanninde tīrātta dāhamāyi
tēngunna karaḷinnu kaivalya mūrttiyāyi
sarva charāchara jīvannum ammayāyi
satyamāyi vāzhunna mātā amṛtēśvari

Immortal Goddess, our eyes that continually shed tears are always thirsting to see You. You liberate us from the suffering in our hearts. You are the mother of all things and You are the eternal truth.

Ā pāda patmattil archanā puṣpamāyi
arppaṇam chēykayāṇ aṭiyanṭe janmavum
puṇchiri tūkī nin māṛōṭu pulkavē
puṇyamāyi tīrkkanē ente janmam

This insignificant one surrenders his life as a flower offered at Your sacred feet. Draw me close and embrace me. Kindly make this birth of mine a blessed one.

BANDA KṚṢṆA

Banda kṛṣṇa chandadinda banda nōde
gōpa vṛndadindā nandisuta banda nōdē

Krishna has come and he spreads happiness and cheer. He enjoys the company of his devotees, the gopas.

Gōvamēva nīva dēva banda nōde
dēvatā vādyagaḷinda banda nōde

Krishna, who carefully tends to the cows, has come with his divine instruments.

Pāpa pōpa gōpa rūpa banda nōde
tāpa lōpa lēpa lōpa banda nōde

The one who removes our sins has come as Gopa. He removes our anger and our defects.

Bhūsura sukha sūsutā banda nōde
vāsudēva vithalatā bandha nōde

Krishna has come spreading divine and earthly pleasures. Vasudeva Vittala Himself has come.

BARAḌĀDA HṚDAYAKE

Baraḍāda hṛdayake śītala dhāreya
eredu jīvita phalavāgi māṭalu
bāramma tāyē lōkamātē
vandisuvē nā ammā ammā
ena baligē nī bārammā

O Mother, please pour forth cool rain on my dry heart. May my life blossom. My dear Mother, I bow down before You, please appear before me.

Baruvalu ammā bandē baruvalu
āseyallī mana nōḍutitē
illa nannammā illa nā endigu
ninnannu agali hōgalārē

My heart hopefully chants the following phrase as if it were a mantra: "Mother will come before me today." "My darling child, I will never be away from you."

BHAKTI KORLE AMMA

Bhakti korle amma
enklegu śakti korle amma

O Mother, grant to us devotion. O Mother, grant us strength.

Īren tūvare śakti korle
edde kēnare bhakti korle
eddeda panare enklegu mātā
Bhakti korle ammā
enklegu śakti korle ammā

Give us the ability to see You, Mother. Grant us devotion to hear and speak what is good. Give us strength, Mother.

Īren neneperē bhakti korle
edde malpare śakti korle
īrena pādogu śaraṇ āvere
Bhakti korle ammā
enklegu śakti korle amma

Please grant us devotion to remember You, Mother. Grant us devotion so that we take refuge at Your feet! Give us devotion and strength, Mother.

Īrē gatiyammā enklegu śakti korle ammā
īrē enklegu bhakti korle amma

You alone are our refuge. Give us strength and devotion, Mother.

Śakti korle
bhakti korle

Grant us strength and devotion.

BHAVĀNI BHĀGYAVIDHĀTRĪ

Bhavāni bhāgyavidhātrī
śivāni śōkanihantrī
mahēśi maṅgaladhātrī
namōstutē giriputrī

Goddess, wife of Bhava (lord Shiva), You determine the fate of those who worship You. Shivani, destroyer of sorrow, great goddess, auspicious Mother, salutations to You, the daughter of the mountain.

Ambē jagadambē jagadambē jai jai mā
ambē jagadambē jagadambē jai jai mā

Victory to Mother, the Mother of the universe!

Śaśānka śēkhara jāyē
surēndra vandita pādē
trilōka pālana nipunē
trinētrabhūṣita vadanē

Wife of the lord who wears the moon (lord Shiva), Your feet are worshipped by the celestials. You skillfully protect all of the three worlds and Your face is adorned with three eyes.

Manōharē mṛduhāsē
parātparē karuṇārdrē
śiva priyē vimalāngē
kṛpānidhē kalayēham

You are beautiful and Your face is adorned with a soft smile. Supreme one, Your heart melts with compassion. Auspicious one, Your body is unblemished and You are a treasure house of sympathy. I meditate on You.

Umē mahēśvara dayitē
ramē surārchita charanē
śivē subhaprada charitē
bhajē bhavāmaya haraṇē

Goddess Uma, wife of lord Shiva, You grant happiness and Your feet are worshipped by the immortals. Auspicious Goddess, Your story sanctifies those who hear it. You remove the sorrow of our life in this world. I worship You.

Namōstutē lalitāmbē
jayōstutē jagadambē
samasta maṅgala rūpē
varapradāyini vandē

Prostrations to Lalitambika; victory to the Mother of the universe. Your form is the abode of all that is auspicious. Granter of boons, I salute You.

BŌLŌ ŚYĀM RĀDHĒ

Bōlō śyām rādhē rādhē
rādhē rādhē śyām
bhav sāgara kō pār karāyē
śyām jī kā nām

Sing the name of Radha and Shyam. Singing Krishna's divine name will enable us to cross the ocean of transmigration.

Vṛndāvana mathurā nahī kēval unkā dhām
bhaktōm kē hṛdaya mē vō kartē he viśrām
būkhē he bas bhāv kē bhāv hō niṣkām
dil sē pukārō āyēngē tvō prabhu dayānidhān
prēm sē bhaj lē ab tū manvā rādhē rādhē śyām

Vrindavan and Mathura are not the only places where Krishna resides. He also lives in the hearts of His devotees. He is hungry for hearts full of dispassion, love and reverence. The compassionate one will hear the call from your heart. O my mind, sing the name of Radhe and Shyam with love.

Sūr mīrā sabnē pāyī ānanda kā dhām
lēnā kabhī na bhūlē vō giridhāri kā nām
un charaṇōm kō pāyē binā na karnā tū ārām
dhanya bhanā dē apnā jīvan bhaj lē rādhē śyām
prēm sē bhaj lē ab tho manvā rādhē rādhē śyām

The great saints Soordas and Meera attained the state of bliss by never forgetting to chant the name of Giridhari. Do not rest until attaining refuge at His feet. Make Your life blessed by chanting the name Radhe Shyam. O my mind, sing the name of Radhe and Shyam with love.

CHANDRA BHĀGA TĪRĪ UBHĒ

Chandra bhāga tīrī ubhē viṭṭēvaṛi
kēśavā murāri jai pāṇḍuranga hari

On the banks of the river Chandrabhaga, standing on an elevation and waiting is Lord Krishna, Murari, Panduranga Hari.

Taṭastha karamana dhyān pāṇḍuranga hari
jap sadā pāvana nām pāṇḍuranga hari
jñaniyāntsā jīvan āhē pāṇḍuranga hari
bhaktāntsā prēmaḷa āhē pāṇḍuranga hari

O my mind, meditate on Panduranga. Repeat His purifying name. Make it an integral part of everything that you do. The Lord Panduranga loves and protects His devotees.

Pāṇḍuranga mani pāṇḍuranga dhyāni
manāt rē gajar pāṇḍuranga vāṇi
kaṣṭa hāraṇa karī pāṇḍuranga hari
bhava sindhu tāraṇa karī pāṇḍuranga hari

Panduranga is in my mind, He pervades my thoughts. I repeat the name of Panduranga, that name which removes hardships and helps one to cross over the ocean of ignorance.

Jay jay vithala pāṇḍuranga
(jay hari vithala pāṇḍuranga)
Śrī hari vithala pāṇḍuranga
(narahari vithala pāṇḍuranga)
Jay śri ranga pāṇḍuranga
(ātmāranga pāṇḍuranga)
Makara kundala pāṇḍuranga
(kaṇthikaustubha pāṇḍuranga)
Śyāma sundara pāṇḍuranga
(sukhānche sāgar pāṇḍuranga)
Trilōka nātha pāṇḍuranga
(paṇdarī nāthā pāṇḍuranga)

Victory to Panduranga, the Lord of humans, who resides in His heavenly abode and is established in His own Self. With a beautiful dark complexion and wearing an attractive earing, Panduranga is an ocean of bliss. He is the Lord of the three worlds.

Nityānanda paramānanda
atmānanda pāṇḍuranga

Panduranga is the eternal supreme bliss of the Self.

Pāṇḍuranga hari jay jay
pāṇḍuranga hari

Victory to Panduranga.

CĒN MILĒ

Cēn milē ārām milē
śānti ōr viśṛām milē
vō hē mā kī gōd vimal
jahā bhaktōm kō prēm milē

One finds calm and relief there; one finds peace and rest. In the lap of the Mother; there is found pure love.

Snigdha snēha apār milē
karuṇā aparampār milē
vō hē mā kā hṛdaya kamal
jahā hari ōm kār milē

One finds unlimited love and affection there. One finds unparalleled compassion. That is the lotus of Mother's heart. That is where you find the Supreme, the primal sound of "OM."

Duḥkh dard santāp miṭē
ādhi vyādhi abhiśāp miṭē
vō hē mā kā hṛday chaman
jahā kān ṭō kā uttāp miṭē

Sorrow, pain, suffering and all ills of the mind and body are removed there. That is the garden of Mother's heart where one is relieved of the agony caused by the thorns of life.

Lōbh mōha sē trāṇ milē
kām krōdh kō virām milē
vō hē mā kā hṛday gagan
jahā gangā kī dhār milē

Mother's expansive heart will rescue us from desire and greed, lust and anger. We will be sanctified as if we had bathed in the river Ganges.

CĒTULETTI

Cētuletti vēṭukonēdā chēyi vadalakammā
centa nilichi dāri chūpi dariki chērchavammā

Mother, I pray with joined palms, don't let go of my hand. Stay with me, show me the way and lead me to the goal.

Paniki rāṇi pūvunu nēnu - ōyammā
vāsana lēdu varṇṇamu lēdu
yōgulaina endarō pillalu nīkaina
maruvukammā ennaṭu nannu

You have so many capable and talented children. Don't forget this child of Yours who is a useless flower devoid of fragrance and color.

Nīvu tappa evaru lēru - māyammā
nīvē nannu nirādariñchitē
gati ēti ī pillaku nīvēnu śaraṇu nāku
maruvukammā ennaṭu nannu

O Amma, I don't have anyone else other than You. If You don't show concern to me then what will I do? You are my only refuge. Please don't leave me.

Japamu rāṇi pillanu ammā - vinavammā
tapamu teliyaka tallaḍillēnu
telisi teliyaka chēsina
tappulu nā veñchaku
manniñchu ennaṭu nannu

Mother, please listen, I am struggling without any proper knowledge of mantra repetition or austerities. Please pardon this child of Yours who has made so many mistakes both knowingly and unknowingly.

CHIDĀNANDA GŌVINDA MUKUNDA

Chidānanda gōvinda mukundā
nandanandana vṛndāvana chandra
dayārūpa dēvēśa murārē
gōpa bālakā gōpīmana chōra

O Krishna, You are the embodiment of consciousness and bliss. Son of Nanda, You are the moon that shines on Vrindavan. Embodiment of compassion, Lord of the Gods, O Vishnu, You have stolen the hearts of the gopis.

Harēkṛṣṇa rādhā hṛdayēśā
kṛṣṇa kṛṣṇa kālindītaṭavāsā

O Krishna, Lord of Radha's heart, You reside on the banks of the Yamuna River.

Prabhāpūrṇṇa pitaṁbaradhārī
vāsudēva māyā mānuṣa vēṣā
ramākānta rājīva dalākṣā
rāsa lōla līlādēha manōjñā

Fully radiant one, wearing a yellow garment, O Krishna, Your human form is a product of Your own Maya. Beloved of Lakshmi, Your eyes are as beautiful as lotus petals. The body You have assumed captivates one and all.

Kālānātha kāvyādi vinōdā
śyāma varṇṇa vamśīnādavilīnā
sudhāvarṣa vēdānta vihārī
sundarāmga vandē gōpajanēśā

Lord of the arts, enjoying poetic works, of dark complexion, absorbed in playing the flute, You shower nectar on all. Handsome one, You abide in the principle of non-duality, O Lord of the gopis.

CHINNA KAṆṆĀ

Kaṇṇā kaṇṇā amma pāṭum
pāṭṭai kēṭṭa tuyilvāy kaṇṇā

My dear Kanna, let mother sing You a lullaby and put You to sleep!

Chinna kaṇṇā entan chella kaṇṇā
solu kaṇṇā entan chuṭṭi kaṇṇā
chinnanchira kaṇkalka tūkkam vantatō
koñcham tūnka kaṇṇā nanṭrāy tūnka kaṇṇā

O darling, innocent Kanna, sleep has come to Your small eyes. Go to sleep, Kanna!

Nāl muzhatum vilayāṭṭu pōtum kaṇṇā
untan piñchu pādam nontiṭumē tūnku kaṇṇā
nāl muzhutum kuzhalūti tilayttāy kaṇṇā
untan chinnakaikaḷ sol kirata tunku kaṇṇā

All day long You ran and played but now Your baby feet may ache. Please go to sleep. All day long You caressed Your flute, and now Your tender hands are saying that You should fall asleep.

Nāl muzhutum enkal manam kavarntāy kaṇṇā
untan chinna kaṇkal sollu kirata tunku kaṇṇā
ulagattai sirittu sirittu mayakkum kaṇṇā
untan sevidazhgaḷ sollu kirata tunku kaṇṇā

All day long You stole our hearts; now those innocent eyes say that You should sleep, Kanna! All day long You entertained the world with Your laughter, but now those baby lips are saying to fall asleep.

Vānattil kārmēgam suzhntat kaṇṇā
anta mēgam kūḍa tālāṭṭu pāṭatu kaṇṇā
alai alaiyāy yamunainadi pāṭatu kaṇṇā
ata salasalavena tālāṭṭu pāṭatu kaṇṇā

The dark clouds have slowly gathered in the sky, Kanna! Even they are singing lullabies to You. The waves of the Yamuna sing to the lapping, gentle lullaby of the river.

Nandavana malar chūḍi ninṭrāy kaṇṇā
nī oli vīśi tikazhkinṭrāy tūnku kaṇṇā
tenṭralilē untan ūñchal āṭatu kaṇṇā
koñcham tūnku kaṇṇā nīyum tūnku kaṇṇā

The flowers from the garden have exhilarated You, Kanna! The evening breeze has come to rock You to sleep.

Nanda gōpa nin bālan yaśōdāvin kaṇṇā
inta pārmuzhutum pāṭatu tālāṭṭu (2x)
ārārī rārō rārī rārī rārī rārō
lōkanāthā nī kaṇ uranku (2x)
ārārī rārō rārī rārī rārī rārō

Darling of Yashoda and Nanda, the whole world is singing a lullaby to You. O protector of the entire world, won't You please sleep?

CHITTAMENUM

Chittamenum sirayinilē
vaṭṭamiṭum paṛavayai pōl
sikkinānkaḷ tavikkirōm – ammā
kāttiṭuvāy

Like an imprisoned bird that flies in circles in its cage, so too are we trapped and suffering in the prison of our minds. O Mother, please save us.

Śivajñāna kalayai nī
enkalku bōdhippāy
chitrinba siṛayilirundu
viṭutalai aḷittiṭuvāy

Please awaken the supreme knowledge within us; free us from the prison of sensual pleasures.

Aḷavillā un anbē
ennālum uṇmaiyenṭrē
enkal manam nāṭi ninṭrē
unnaṭi sērndiṭumē

Your boundless love is a manifestation of the supreme truth. Knowing that, our seeking minds will merge into Your feet.

Ēṇippaṭi pōle un anbum
ānatuvē ēṛinānkaḷ
aṭaivōmē nin tiruvaṭimalarē

Your love is a ladder to the supreme consciousness. Climbing that ladder, we will attain Your lotus feet.

CHŌḌ DĒ MANSĒ

Chōḍ dē mansē duḥkha kī chintā
nit yē sumir tū satya rē
dēh tū nahī man bhī tū nahī
tū he ātmā jān lē

Give up thoughts of sorrow and remember always that you are the Truth. You are neither the body nor the mind, know that you are the Atman (Self).

Hār gayā tū khōj mē sukh kē
is jag kē sab bhōg mē
paramānanda he tērē antar
kabhī vahām tō jhāmk rē

In the attempt to find a lasting happiness through indulgence in material pleasures alone you have met with defeat. The undying happiness is within you, that is where it should be sought.

Mē tum kē is bhēd mē manvā
nahī he śānti jān lē
ēk hī ātmā sab mē he tū
hī sab mē he vyāpt rē

Know that as long as you entertain the thought of "I" and "you" as separate entities then you will never know peace. The same consciousness is in all beings, the inner essence in you pervades all others.

Ātma sāmrājya kā tū he mālika
manvā tū kabhī dīn nahī
paramśakti kā srōt bhī tū he
manvā tū kam sōr nahī

You are the master of the kingdom of the Self; you are never poor. Neither are you weak; you are the source of supreme power.

CHŌṬO CHŌṬO GĀYĪ

Chōṭo chōṭo gāyī chōṭo chōṭo gaudō
chōṭṭottā bhittōre mo madona gōpāl

A herd of little cows and a group of little cowherd boys, my enchanting little Gopal is with them.

Gāso khāyē gāyī dūttō piyē gaudō
lōhōṇī khāyē mōrō madona gōpāl

The cows eat the grass, the cowherd boys drink the milk, and my little Gopal eats the butter.

Āgē āgē gāyī pochē pochē gaudā
motdīrē chālē mōrō madona gōpāl

The cows go in front, the little cowherds come behind, and my little Gopal is in the middle.

Chōṭṭō chōṭṭō hāttōrē chōṭṭō chōṭṭō bādhi
bōyinsi bajāyē mō madona gōpāl

Little pieces of sticks in their small pairs of hands, my enchanting Gopal plays the flute.

Chōṭṭō chōṭṭō sakhā sakhi madhubaṇa mēlā
rāsa rachāye mōrā madona gōpāl

Little female companions and the boy of Vrindavan, my little Gopal enchants everyone with His divine drama.

DAR DAR MĒ

Dar dar mē bhaṭaktā rahā
mansil kahā nahī thā patā
arth milā is jīvan kō
jab mā tērē śaraṇā āyā

I was wandering from place to place having no idea where my destination was. But when I took refuge in You, Mother, this life became meaningful.

Kōṭi pranāṁ kōṭi praṇām
śatakōṭi pranāṁ ammā

Salutations to You, hundreds of millions of salutations to You, Amma!

Ās bharā thā is mana mē
kisī apnē kā intasār thā
tum hō mērē jō tūnē kahā
nahi mē anāth ehsās huvā

This heart was eagerly waiting for someone to claim it as their own. When You uttered, "You are mine," I realized that I am no longer an orphan.

Itnā kuch hē diyā tū nē
tujhē dēnē kō mā kuch bhī nahī
hē arppit ye mērā jīvan
śrī charaṇō mē mā amṛtēśvarī

You have given me so much. But I have nothing to give You in return. I surrender this life at Your sacred feet, O Immortal Goddess!

DĪP KA NĀ

Dīp ka nā jānū bātī nā jānū
anḍiyārē van mē kōyī rāh nā jānū

I know no light and I know no lamp; in this dark forest I cannot see the path before me.

Dēvī mā tū mērī mā tērē sivā nā kōyī mā
tērē sivā nā kōyī mā tērē sivā nā kōyī mā

O my Divine Mother, I have no one but You. Mother, I have no one but You!

Nāv na jānū kēvaṭa nā jānū
is bhav sāgara mē kōyī pār na jānū
jānū bas ik lakṣya mā
jānū bas ik lakṣya mā
dēvī mā tū mērī mā

I know neither boat nor boatman; I don't know where lies the shore of this ocean of birth and death. I know only that my goal is You, my Divine Mother!

Sansār nā jānū banḍu nā jānū
ik tērē sivā mai kuch ōr nā jānū
jānū bas ik satya mā
jānū bas ik ās mā
dēvī mā tū mērī mā

I don't know this world; I know no kith or kin. I know nothing but You. I know only one truth, one aspiration, Mother, O my Divine Mother!

DUKHATTĪ JVĀLAYIL

Dukhattī jvālayil kattikkariyumen
chittattilēkaṇē snēham
muktiku pātram alenkilum nin prēma
bhaktikku kāḷunnu dāham

Give some love to this heart that is burning in the fire of sorrow! I am not fit for liberation; I simply thirst for love and devotion to You.

Viṅgunnu mānasam tiṅgunna śōkattāl
maṅgunnu kaṇṇukaḷammē
muṅgātī jīvita naukayiteṅgane
taṅgunnu nin kālmunambil

My heart throbs with grief and my eyes have become feeble. How can I keep the boat of my life afloat at Your feet?

Nin snēha sinduvil binduvāy tīruvān
vembukayāṇente svāntam
andhakārāvṛtam en manadyōvilor
ambiḷiyāy vannudikkū

My heart yearns to become a drop in the ocean of Your love. Please rise up as the moon in the dark sky of my mind!

Mādhuryam tiṅgumā vāṅmaya tīrthattin
ōlattālullam tazhukū
snēhāmṛtamūṭṭi ōmkārasārārtha
sāndrāva bōdham teḷikkū

Kindly caress and cool my heart with the holy water of Your sweet words! Feed me the nectar of Your love and awaken in me a deep awareness of the Supreme.

ENKIRUNTU VANDŌM

Enkiruntu vandōm
etai koṇṭu vandōm
enatenṭru kūṛiṭavē
etai izhandu ninṭrōm

Where do we come from? What have we brought with us? What do we lose and why do we call it our own?

Edanai ichittōm
epporulil patruvaittōm
pār tanil kaṭṭuṇṭu
paritavittu ninṭrōm

What have we wished for and felt attachment to? Regret has arisen as a result of having bound ourselves to what is perishable.

Enkiruntō vandān
enai kāṇ entrān
īrēzhulakilum
iruppavan nān enṭrān

When the Lord comes amongst us He teaches us to perceive Him and the world correctly. Thus we come to see Him pervading the universe.

Avanai kaṇṭa pinbō
akattinil nikazhntatenna
āṇṭavan avanarulāl
aṟiyāmai nīnkappetrēn

After having seen His universal form there are no words to describe what has happened to me. By His Grace my ignorance has been eradicated.

ENNICHA TANNE

Ennicha tanne ninnichayennōtuvān
ennenikākkumenammē
ennaṟivu ninnaṟivil ninnu
viṭarunnuvennennu chollīṭuvānākum

Mother, when will I be able to say that my wish is the same as Your wish? When will I be able to assert that what I know actually blossoms forth from Your knowledge?

En kriyakal nin chuvaṭu kaṇṭu tuṭarum
pulariyennu teḷiyum munnilammē
ichayām śaktiyum jñānamām śaktiyum
kriyayenna śaktiyum nīyē

When will that day dawn when my actions will follow in Your footsteps? You alone are the powers of will, action and knowledge, Mother.

Ninnil ninnallāteyennil ninnuṇarunna
tonnumillaṛiyunnu ṭayē ñān
enkilum ninnartha garbhamām dṛṣṭiyil
en mukham tāzhnnu pōkunnu

O Mother, isn't it true that nothing arises in me that doesn't come from You? Then why am I unable to withstand it when Your profound gaze penetrates deeply into my soul.

Ninnōla muyaruvānāvāttorī
bhūmiyente pātāḷamākunnu
en lōkamāṇu nin lōkamennōtuvān
ennenikkākum en ammē

From the mundane realm of my material existence, I cannot rise to Your divine heights. This earth is but a netherworld for me. When will I be able to claim that my world and Your world are one and the same, O Mother?

Amṛtēśvarī sakala hṛdayēśvarī
Jaya jaya jaya jaya

Victory to the immortal Goddess, the Goddess of the heart.

ENTĒ ENNAMMĒ

Entē ennammē innariyān amāntamen
santāpanāśini vandē jaganmayi
vallāte ñāninnu allal koṇṭurūkunnu
vallāyma māttuvān vannīṭukambikē

Why, O Mother, is there a delay in merging in You? Salutations to You, universal Mother. You are the remover of all sorrows. I am suffering greatly; kindly come to relieve me of my sorrows.

Varūkillē nallorū chinta pōlinnum
varamillā pāzhtapassāṇō ī janmam
tamassēnti tamassēnti manassāke aṭayunnu
uṣassē nī uṣassē nī varūkillē nī

Won't even one good thought arise within me? Is my life just a wasted austerity that brings no benefit? My mind is immersed in the darkness that I carry as a burden. Will You not come within me as the dawn?

Karakaṇākaṭalil ñān kaṭalāsutōṇipōl
tiramāla kūṭayunnu āzhttil aṭiyunnu
vazhiyillē ammē ī chuzhiyil ninnēṟuvān
aṇayillē ammē ī azhalil ninnēttuvān

I am no more than a paper boat in the boundless ocean. The waves toss me here and there and I sink to the depths. Is there no way to escape from this whirlpool? O Mother, hasn't the time come for You to lift me up out of this misery?

Karaḷ tēṅikkarayunnu kadanam nirayunnu
karuṇārdra mānasē kṛpayillē tellum
azhalinte koṭumvaḷḷi viṭu vichu pōrūvān
aṟivillennammē nī tanne śaraṇam

I cry with a grief-stricken heart. O compassionate Mother, don't You feel even a little mercy for me? I don't know how to free myself from the clutches of crazy sorrow. You are my only refuge, Mother.

GAJAI KAṬṬI

Gajai kaṭṭi ōṭi ōṭi bārō
emma kamala nayana kuṇintu kuṇintu bārō
ninna puṭṭapāda hṛṭuki hṛṭuki nāvu
ninna divyanāma hāṭi hāṭi bandevu

O Krishna, endowed with lotus shaped eyes, tie on Your anklets and come running and dancing. Searching for Your tender feet we have come singing the divine names.

Dēvakī nandana rādhā jīvana
kēśavā hare mādhavā
pūtana marddana pāpa vināśana
kēśavā hare mādhavā
gōkula bālane ōṭi bārō
gōpāla bālane kuṇintu bārō

Devaki's son, the very life of Radha, Hare, Madhava, slayer of Putana, destroyer of sins, child of Gokula, cowherd boy, come running and dancing.

Kamsa vimarddana kāliya narttana
kēśavā hare mādhavā
āśrita vatsala āpat bāndhavā
kēśavā hare mādhavā
ōmkāra nādamē ōṭi bārō
ānanda gītamē kuṇintu bārō

Slayer of Kamsa, the dancer upon the serpent Kaliya's head, Keshava, Hare, Madhava, You are affectionate to Your devotees. You protect those in danger, O embodiment of "OM." Come running and dancing.

Pāṇdava rakṣaka pāpavināśana
kēśavā hare mādhavā
arjuna rakṣaka ajñāna nāśakā
kēśavā hare mādhavā
gītāmṛtamē ōṭi bārō
hṛdayānandamē kuṇintu bārō

Protector of the Pandavas, destroyer of sins, Keshava, Hare, Madhava, O protector of Arjuna, destroyer of ignorance, You are the nectar of the Gita. Bliss of the heart, come running and dancing.

GAṆANĀTHANIN ARUL

Gaṇanāthanin arul vēṇṭiṭuvōm
kavalaikal yāvum tīrntiṭavē
nāḷum gaṇanāthanin aruḷ vēṇṭiṭuvōm

Let us constantly pray for the blessings of lord Ganesha to vanquish all of our worries.

Ōm enum mandira vaṭivai koṇṭavanē
ōtum maraipporuḷil ōnki nirppavanē
akila ulakirkum ādhāram nīyantrō
aṭiyavar manatinil nimmati niraintiṭavē

Lord Ganesha, You are the embodiment of the mantra "OM." You are featured most prominently in the Vedas; for the entire universe You form the firm foundation. Those who worship You find their hearts filled with peace.

Vēzha mukham kaṇṭāl vēdanai tīrntiṭumē
vēṇṭum varankalai vēṇṭāmal tarumbavanē
umaiyavaḷ maintanē un aruḷ nāṭukiṛōm
punnagai mukhatōṭu puvi tannai kāttiṭavē

You fulfill all of our desires without even being asked to do so. When we behold Your elephant face our sorrows vanish. Son of Parvati, we seek that You, with Your smiling face, should grant Your blessings of protection for this Earth.

GAṆĒŚĀYA NAMAḤ ŌM

Gaṇēśāya namaḥ ōm ganēśāya namaḥ
jay jay jay gaṇēśāya namaḥ ōm

I bow to Lord Ganesha; Victory to Him.

Guṇa gān tēri sun hē gaṇēśā
kṛpānidhi tum sab kē īśā
dīn bandhu tum jag kē trātā
pārvati nandana ṣaṇ mukha bhrātā

Listen to these praises that I am singing for You, O Lord Ganesha. Treasure house of compassion, You are the Lord of all. You are a friend to those who are in need. Savior of the world, son of the Goddess Parvati, You are the elder brother of Muruga.

Tum hō prabhu guṇ jñān kē sāgar
sur muni man mē nit ujāgar
karū prasanna mē kēsē nāthā
prēm bhakti sab sukh kē dātā

O Lord, You are an ocean of virtue and knowledge. Forever You burn radiantly in the hearts of the sages. You bestow true devotion and all well-being upon us. What can I do to please You?

Mērē man mē ab ēk hī āśā
ēk hī ās daras kō pyāsā
hṛdaya kamal tērī ōj mē phūlē
miṭē andhiyārā man mōj mē jhūlē

Only one wish remains in my mind. I have only one desire. I long to see You. May the lotus of my heart bloom in Your light. May darkness be dispelled and may my mind dance in joy.

GŌPĀLA NACHŌ

Gōpāla nachō nachō gōkula bālā
gōvinda bōlō bōlō vēṇuvilōlā
giridhārī gāvō gāvō naṭavaralālā
vanamālī dhimi dhimi rāsavilōlā

Dance, O Gopala, O cowherd boy. O Gopala, who plays the flute, sing! You lifted up the mountain, O great dancer. Wearing a garland of wildfowers, You revel in the rasa dance.

Muralī dhara mukunda mādhava
manamōhana mathuranātha
nandalālā navanīta chōrā
śyāma varṇṇā sundarabālā

O Krishna, holding the flute, You steal the hearts of one and all, O Lord of Mathura, darling of Nanda, You captivate the minds of all beings in creation, O beautiful child of a dark complexion!

Madhusūdana gītānāyaka
Śrīrādhā vallabha kṛṣṇa
yamunātaṭ kuñjavihārī
hē yādava yadukula nāthā

You killed the great demon, Madhu; teacher of the celstial song, Radha, Krishna, You play in the foliage along the banks of the river Yamuna. You are the Lord of the Yadu clan in which You were born.

Nārāyaṇa naraharirūpā
vasudēva natajanapālā
śrī kṛṣṇa śrī hari kṛṣṇa
gōpī jana hṛdaya vihārā

O Lord, You protect those who have no other refuge than You. O auspicious Lord Vishnu, You play in the hearts of the gopis.

GŌVARDHANA DHARA

Gōvardhana dhara gōkula nandana
gōpī janapriya gōpari pālaka
kēśava mādhava yādava mōhana
muralī mukundā murārē
murārē murārē murārē murārē

You lifted the Govardhana mountain, O son of Gokul, You are loved by the gopis. Born in the Yadava clan, beautiful one, Your presence graces all of the cows, O Krishna.

Mērē kanhā mērē kanhā
ājāvō hē nanda dulārā

My Krishna, Nanda's son, please come before me.

Mākhan churānē kanhā
ānā chupkē sē mērē dhār
na karnā mujhkō tum udās ō pyārē
ṭhumak ṭhumak chalat chalat āvō kanhayyā āj

Come to steal butter from my house. Do not disappoint me, dear Krishna, come before me today.

Atbhuta hē līla tērī
mahimā tērī hē apār
tarsē hē nayanā daras kō tērē
rās rachānē ranga jamānē āvō kanhayyā āj

Mysterious is Your divine play and infinite is Your greatness. My eyes long for the sight of You. Come before me today and dance and play with me.

HARI GŌPĀLĀ HARI GŌPĀLĀ

Hari gōpālā hari gōpālā (4x)

O Lord, Gopala.

Kāyāmbuvarṇṇā nin smaraṇayāl manam nīla
kaṭambu vṛkṣam pōle taḷiraṇiññīṭunnu

O Krishna, beautiful is Your dark blue complexion. Remembering You, my mind bears tender new leaves like a blue kadamba tree.

Mukiloli maṇivarṇṇan mṛdu pāda sparśattālen
manassoru vṛndāvaniyāy māttukillē kaṇṇā
ivaluṭe janmam ennum amṛtasvarūpanām nin
vanamālayil kōrtta tulsi pōlākaṇam
hari gōpālā hari gōpālā

O Kanna, Your complexion equals that of the dark blue clouds. Won't You turn my mind into a Vrindavan with the soft touch of Your feet? O Lord, let my life forever be like a tulsi leaf in the wild flower garland worn by You. You are the immortal one.

Kāruṇya pūruṣanām nin tiru mizhikaḷen
hṛttilē tāpamellām akattīṭaṇē kaṇṇā
janma sāphalyām ēkum nin rūpam darśikkuvān
ivaluṭe nētraṅgaḷe anugrahikkū kaṇṇā
hari gōpālā hari gōpālā

O Kanna, You are the embodiment of compassion. May the glance from Your divine eyes remove all the sorrows in my heart. Bless my eyes so that I may have the vision of Your form. That vision bestows the ultimate fulfillment of this human birth.

HĒ KṚPĀMAYĪ AMBĒ

Hē kṛpāmayī ambē
hē dayāmayī dēvī

O compassionate Mother, O compassionate goddess!

Ham hē tērē bachē mā
kṛpā tū ham par kar nā mā
ek yahi āśā hē mā
isē tū purā kar nā mā

I am Your child! Give me Your grace, mother! That is my only wish. Kindly fulfill that wish, mother!

Dard bharā jīvan hē mā
dard miṭhānē vālī tū
jal dī ākar jīvan mē
barsānā tū amṛta sadā

This life is full of pain, mother! You are here to remove that pain. Come quickly into my life and shower Your eternal grace always!

Pyār sē ham kō pāl nā mā
rāh dikhānā ham kō mā
tērē charaṇō mē mayyā
bas jāyē ham jal dī mā

Protect us with Your love, Mother! Show us the way! Without any further delay grant us a permanent place at Your feet, O Mother!

HĒ MAIYĀ TŪ

Mā jay mā mā jay mā
jay jay mā jay mā jay mā
mā jay mā mā jay mā
jay jay mā jay mā jay mā

Victory to Mother.

Hē maiyā tū ati pyārī
tū ākar basnā dil mē
tērā hī ēk sahārā
jīnē kā sambhal hamārā

O my dearest Mother, please come to me and live inside my heart. You are my only support. You are the only strength of my life.

Sumiran tērā kartē he
dhyān tērā hī dhartē he
miṭ tē he us sē sārē
kaṭ tē he duḥkh hamārē

By constantly remembering You and meditating upon You, all of our sorrows are destroyed.

Vinatī yē sun lē maiyā
apnālē hamkō jaldī
tērē hī ēk bharōsā
jītē ham tērē bachē

Please listen to this request, O Mother. Hasten to make all of us Your own. You are the only hope that is held dear in the life of Your children.

HṚDAYA PUṢPAVĒ

Hṛdaya puṣpavē hēlu nin
nayana toyda jalayāvudu
duḥkha bāṣpavō ānanda bāṣpavō
jēnō prēmarasavō

Flower of my heart, please tell me why you shed these tears. Are they tears of sorrow or tears of joy? Are they honey? Are they the essence of love?

Anubhūtigala madhurasmṛtiyali
hṛdayavāyitē amṛta
hēḷu nayana neneda kāraṇa
vichārava mānasamalare

Do the tears arise from the bliss that emanates from the memory of our divine experiences? Tell me, flower of my heart, why you shed these tears.

Ī MANŌJÑA BHŪMIYIL

Ī manōjña bhūmiyil jīva gangā dhārayil
nīntivanna dēvalōka rāja hamsa vāhini
en manassil tānuvanna śānti dūtiyāṇu nī
śānti dūtiyāṇu nī

You are the Goddess from Heaven. Seated upon Your swan, You came swimming on the celestial river to this beautiful world. You bring peace to the inner core of my mind.

Sāma gāna mālapikkum āzhiyalakaḷ pōlum
ātma harṣa nirvṛtiyil līnamāya pōle
nin chiritan manjimayil nīntiyāṭi nīḷe
nīntiyāṭi nīḷe

The waves of the ocean chant the Omkara mantra, the sound that merges with the bliss of the Self. In the sweetness of Your smile the waves dance.

ūnamezhā jñāna vāypil ūzhi kākkum ammē
sīmayezhā snēhavāypil tēṅga lāttum ammē
en manassin kalviḷakkil dhyēya dīpamāṇu nī
dhyēya dīpamāṇu nī

With Your endless knowledge, O Mother, You protect this world. With Your limitless love You calm our sobbing hearts. In the lamp of my heart, You are the light upon which I meditate.

dāha hṛittaṭam taṇukke nī kaniññu peyyavē
snēha dhārayil kutirnnu ñānaliññu tīravē
mēdinī hṛdantamām hṛdam tuḷumbiṭunnitā
hṛdam tuḷumbiṭunnitā

You shower Your grace to cool my burning heart, I am melting in the rain of Your love. The inner core of my heart is flooded with divine love.

INIYENTINĀLASYAM

Iniyentinālasyam iniyentināmayam
iniyentinēkānta neṭuvīrppukaḷ
kaṇṇīrtuṭaykunnor amma tan tāriḷam
kaikaḷil kuññuṅgaḷ nammaḷ

What reason is there for us to continue to feel weary? Why should we be dejected any longer? Where is the need for us to sigh deeply in solitude? We are small babies in the soft arms of the Mother who wipes away the tears of all.

Kaṇṇunīr kaṇikakaḷ malarāki māttiṭām
amma tannōmalkazhalil
gadgadaṅgaḷ mahita mantraṅgaḷākiṭām
amma tan nāma smṛtiyil

At Mother's holy feet, let us transform our tears into flowers. Let our halting and broken speech be transmuted into exalted mantras in the remembrance of Mother's divine name.

Ariyāt irikunnuvenkilum akaneññi
larivāyirikunnitamma
oru pūvil oru tuḷḷi madhuram kaṇakkuḷḷil
uṛavāyirikunnitamma

Mother lives in my innermost self as pure existence, though I fail to experience Her as such. She dwells in each flower as the source of every drop of nectar.

Santōṣabharitam parālparē hṛdayattil
nin prēma pada bhakti bhāvam
veṇ tārakam pōle minnunnit eppozhum
nin ormma chintānabhasil

Feeling pure devotion to Your holy feet fills my heart with joy. O Mother, memories of You shine like stars in the clear sky of my thoughts.

ĪŚĀR TUMĪ

Īśār tumī dayā karō
tumī binā kē āchē

O Lord, please show us mercy. Other than You, who is here for us?

Jagat srōṣṭā ō tumī
bināśakāri ō tumī
bipōdē trāṭṭā hō tumī
tumī binā kē āchē

You are the creator and the destroyer of the world. Even misfortune is Your creation. Other than You, who is here for us?

Mātā tumī tumī pitā
bōnḍu tumī tumī ṣōkā
kēbōl tōmāri āsrōy
tumī binā kē āchē

You are our Mother, Father, Benefactor and Friend. You are our only refuge. Other than You, who is here for us?

Nāhī rākhī kōnō khabar
tōmār gūṇō gān chāḍā
jāyē tō ār kōthāy jāyi
tumī binā kē āchē

We don't know anything. Without our love for You, what would become of us? Other than You, who is here for us?

ĪŚORI JOGODĪŚARI

Īśori jogodīśari
poripālini koruṇāmōyi
śāśoto mukti dāyini dukho
hōrō momo jonanī

O Goddess of the universe, You are the preserver and the giver of grace and eternal liberation. Please rid me of all my sorrows.

Ṣoṅsārēl ṣukh dēkhēchi ami
śēśē tārā dukhō dāy
ṣē kōṣṭō mōre diyōnā – ma
ōgnitē pōton goṣomo

I have seen that the pleasures of this worldly life are so full of afflictions. Please do not make me suffer like the moths that fall into the fire.

Kāmonār pāś ṣomukhe mā
morōṇer pāś pośchāttē
duyipāśē bēndhē rākhō mōrē
ekē mōṇ tobo līlā

I am bound by the noose of desire in front of me and the noose of desire behind me, O Mother. What a pity it would be to tie them together.

Pothobhōlā nākkarō nā mōrē
kṛpākorō jonanī
klēśōnāśini śkōbhār momo
ṣokkōlī korōdur

Don't let me wander down the wrong path, O eternal one. Shower Your grace on me. O Mother, the destroyer of misery, remove my burden of sorrow.

Mānōb jonma phalērjōnno
kori āmi prārthonā
sorborūpiṇi mohādēbi
tobopādēkori bōndanā

O Mother of the world, for achieving the fruit of human birth I pray with joined palms. O Goddess of the world, who dwells in all forms, I bow at Your feet.

JAG MĀTĀ

Jag mātā ko dil sē pukāro
ma ka bhajan prēm sē gāvo
mere dil mē maiyya kab āvoge
nāto rothe āsuvon mē dūbjāyēngē

Call out from your heart to the Mother of the universe. Sing songs of the Mother with love. "When will the Divine Mother come into my heart? If She doesn't come, I will drown in a sea of tears."

Tēri ānkhen to dayā ka sāgar hai
tēri bāhon mē mēri mukti hain
tērē āwāz sunkar man mē śānti āye
tērē mukh dekhar dil mē pyār āye

Mother, Your eyes are an ocean of compassion. Within Your arms I find my liberation. When hearing Your voice my mind fills with peace. When I see Your face my heart fills with love.

Are ma ka bhajan zor sē gāvo
bhakti bhavse mak ka pyāra nām bōlō
durga durga bhavāni jaya bhadrakali
munijana pālaki jayatu śivāni

Sing songs to the Mother with your whole heart. With devotion repeat the beloved name of the Mother. "Durga, Durga, Bhavani, victory to Bhadrakali who protects the sages, victory to You, the essence of Shiva."

JAI GŌPĀLAKA

Jai gōpālaka jag hitakārī
jai muralī dhara kunjavihārī
chambi tērī pānē kō pyārī
taras rahē kṛṣṇa murārī

Victory to Gopala, victory to our benefactor! Victory to the one who holds the flute and roams merrily about! O dear Krishna, we are yearning for You.

Kṛṣṇa kṛṣṇa jaya rādhā kṛṣṇa
kṛṣṇa kṛṣṇa manamōhana kṛṣṇa
kṛṣṇa kṛṣṇa muralīdhara kṛṣṇa
kṛṣṇa kṛṣṇa madhurādhipa kṛṣṇa

Victory to Krishna, O captivating Muralidhara (holder of the flute)! Krishna, O Lord of Mathura!

Ham kō darśana dījō giridhara
sankata dūr karō tum manahara
tērē milan kō kyā taṭ pāyē
sudh budh khō ham pagalāyē

Grant to us the vision of Your form, O Krishna. Remove our doubts. We have become agitated in our eagerness to merge in You. We have become crazy!

Jīvan mē yah ēk hi āśā
tum hī hamārā ēk bharōsā
ham kō nirāś karōgē kyā tum
tab karuṇā tum kis par karōgē

All that I desire in my life is to merge in You. You are the only one who can be trusted. Will You reject us? If so, then who is deserving of Your compassion?

Āvō jal dī darśan dē dō
ham kō tum jal dī apanāvō
karuṇāmay hō yah mat bhūlō
karuṇā karkē ham kō ubārō

Come quickly and grant to us the vision of Your form. Make us Yours! You are full of compassion; don't forget that! Show mercy towards us and uplift us!

JAI JAGADAMBĒ AMBĒ MĀTĀ

Jai jagadambē ambē mātā
dhāv jhaṇī āttā
kṛpākarī hē ambē mātā
dhāv gheyī ātā

Victory to the Mother of the universe. Please save us quickly, Mother, bestow Your grace on us.

Jay jaykār jay jaykār
āyī tujhē jay jay kār

Victory to Mother.

Nahī śakti nahī bhakti
jhad kari hṛdayi dhari tū āyī
dhanya jyās mīḷē tujhē darśan
tujhyā charaṇi śata kōṭi vandan

People receive Your grace according to their own faith. Those whose faith allows them to see the vision of You have their life fulfilled. Mother, I offer countless prayers at Your feet.

Dhanya dhanya vhāvē āyī
darśan ghadō ṭhāyī ṭhāyī
tava charaṇi mama prītī tsadhlī
hētsa mājhē bhāgya āyī

It has been my great good fortune to offer some small service at Your feet. Please bless me that I have countless such opportunities in the future.

JAI JAI JAI GAṆANĀTHA GAJĀNANA (PĀHI GAJĀNANA)

Jai jai jai gaṇanātha gajānana
jai jai jai gaṇanātha gajānana

Victory to Ganesha with the elephant face.

Pāhi gajānana parama dayākara
sidhivināyaka svāmi – śiva
parvati priyatanayā
gaṇanāyaka maṅgala śubha sadanā

I take refuge in Ganapati, the God who has assumed the form of an elephant. O supremely compassionate One, destroyer of misfortune, the beloved son of Shiva and Parvati, You are the fountainhead of auspiciousness.

Śāśvata nāda śarīramanōhara
śrī gaṇapati śritapālā
śvētāmbaradhara chidghanarūpā
pādāmbujam abhayam

You are the living embodiment of the eternal sound "Om." Stealer of our hearts, preserver of all that is good, adorned in white garments, O embodiment of pure consciousness, Your blessed feet are my refuge.

Vandita pādā nandita rūpā
vighna vināyaka dēvā
mōdaka hasta amōdaka dāyaka
mām pālaya jagadīśa

Your feet are worthy of worship and Your delightful form is the embodiment of bliss. O Lord, You remove all obstacles and misfortunes. You hold the stuffed dumpling, the modaka, Your favorite food, in Your hand. Kindly protect me, O Lord of the world, giver of joy.

JAI JAI JAI GAṆANĀTH GAJĀNANA

Jai jai jai gaṇanāth gajānana
kaṣṭ harō hamārā

Victory to Ganesha with the elephant face. Please remove all my obstacles.

Riddhi siddhi kē tum hō swāmi
prēma bhakti kē data
andhkār mē dubē man kō
kar dō ab ujiyārā

You are the Lord of prosperity and power, the bestower of love and devotion. Illuminate this mind that is steeped in the darkness of ignorance.

Tujhkō mēra pēhla vandan
bār bār praṇām - gajānana

I bow to You first, I bow again and again.

Rup tēra he kitna pyārā
mā pārvati kē bālā
māna māta pitā jag sārā
param jñān phal pāyā

Your form is so endearing, O son of mother Parvati. You revered Your mother and father as the whole universe and in doing so You received in return the fruit of supreme knowledge.

Gīt pē mērē nācho gaṇapati
bhakt ka dil bharjāyē - gajānana

Dance to this song of mine, O Ganapati, let this devotee's heart be filled with joy.

JAI JAI MĀTĀ

Jai jai mātā jai jagad jananī dēvi mātā
vijayē mātā priyajana pālini vimalē mātā
vīṇāpāṇi vidyādāyini sarasvati mātā
jananī jay jay jagadō dhāriṇi jay jay mātā

Victory to Mother, victory to the Mother of the Universe. Victory to the beloved protector of the people. Victory to Mother Saraswati who holds the veena in Her hand and imparts knowledge. Victory to Mother, the uplifter of the universe.

Dēvi mātā durgē mātā vidyā mātā śaktī mātā
ambē mātā kali mātā jay jay jay
jagadambē mātā jay jagadambē jay jay jay

O divine Mother, Devi, Durga, Kali, bestower of knowledge and power! Victory to You!

Jay jay mātā sundara vadanē mahitē mātā
jay jay mānasa hamsini lasitē varadē mātā
jananī jay jay jagadō dhāriṇi jay jay mātā

Victory to the great divine Mother whose face is beautiful. Victory to the swan that sports in the mind of the yogi, to the one who grants boons. Victory to the one who uplifts the entire world!

Jay jay mātā himagiritanayē pārvati mātā
jay jay hṛdaya nivāsini śrīmayi śubhadē mātā
jananī jay jay jagadō dhāriṇi jay jay mātā

Victory to Devi Parvati, the daughter of Himavat. Victory to the one who resides in the heart, the giver of auspiciousness, the uplifter of the universe!

JAI JAI RĀM

Jai jai rām kṛṣṇa harē
jai jai rām kṛṣṇa harē

Victory to Lord Rama! Victory to Krishna!

Daśaratha nandana rāma namō
vasudēva nandana kṛṣṇa namō

Salutations to Rama, the son of Dasaratha. Salutations to Krishna, the son of Vasudeva.

Sītā vallabha rāma namō
rādhā vallabha kṛṣṇa namō

Salutations to Rama, the Lord of Sita. Salutations to Krishna, the Lord of Radha.

Rāvaṇa mardhana rāma namō
kamsa niṣūdana kṛṣṇa namō

Salutations to Rama who destroyed Ravana. Salutations to Krishna who killed Kamsa.

JAI MĀ BHAVĀNĪ

Jai mā bhavānī jagadambē
jai mā śivānī jagadambē

Victory to Bhavani, victory to Shivani, the Mother of the universe.

Tērē pyār kē ik būnd kē liyē mēnē
chōḍ diyā sansār
nā sukh chāhū nā kuch chāhū - mā
chāhū tō tērā pyār

I have left the dark world behind hoping that I would obtain just one drop of Your immortal love. I desire neither happiness nor anything else; I simply want You to shower Your love on me.

Nanhā hū mē nādān hū
rastōn sē tērē añjān hū
ik tērē pyār kē bal par jiyū
chōḍ na dēnā sāth

I am a small child; I am innocent and unfamiliar with Your ways. I live only for Your love, You must never leave my company.

Ik tū hī bharōsā tūhī sahārā
ik tērē sivā nā kōyī hamārā
rakṣā karō surakṣā mē tērī
jīvan kā hō savērā

You are my one and only faith and my sole support. I have none other than You. Please save me Mother. It is only in Your constant care that the morning of my life will at last dawn.

Jab tērē hō gayē he ham
tō kis bāt kā bhalā hamkō hō gam
jō tērā sāyā hō ham par hardam
jō tērē sahārā hō har ik kadam

I have nothing to be sad about now that I have at last become one of Your own. You will be there right beside me all of the time, and You will be my guide for every step that I take.

JAPŪ MĒ SADĀ

Japū mē sadā hari kā nām
rāt din subhah śyām
rādhē śyām rādhē śyām
kṛṣṇa nām kṛṣṇa nām

Without stopping I chant the name of Hari. Night and day, morning and evening I chant the names of Radhe Shyam and Krishna.

Rādhē śyām kṛṣṇa nām mē gāvū rē
harē rām harē kṛṣṇa nām japū rē
santa sajjana sang mi milu rē
satguru charaṇa pūja bhajan karū rē

I sing the glorious names of Radhe Shyam and Krishna, I chant their names incessantly. Saints and good-hearted, pure people are those that I keep company with. Worshipping the holy feet of the Guru I sing praises to the lord.

Śyām jap nām jap sadā bōlū rē
śrīdhar vāsudēv bhajan karū rē
murali gān mē mi nacho rē
mukundā gōvinda bhajan karū rē

I forever chant Shyam's holy name. I sing praises to Sridhara Vasudeva. I dance when I hear the blissful strains of the lord's flute. I sing the names of Mukunda and Govinda in exaltation.

Madhusūdhana madanamōhana śaraṇa rahū rē
nārāyaṇa nārāyaṇa guṇ gāvu rē
murali gān mē mi nāchū rē
mukundā gōvinda bhajan karū rē

I take refuge in Madhusudana the slayer of Madhu. He is the one who charms the mind of His devotees. I sing praises of the great Narayana, I dance hearing those blissful notes on the flute. I sing the names of Mukunda and Govinda in exaltation.

JŌT JALĀLĒ

Jōt jalālē rām ki manamē
sab viṣayō kō āndhiyārē taj

Keep the effulgent Ram in your heart to eradicate all darkness. Chant Ram, chant the name of Ram alone.

sab rōgōm kī auṣadh rām
har uljhan kī suljhan rāmā
rām rām jay jay rām (2x)
Jab bhī sankaṭ sē ghir jāyē
man pagalē tū rām rām bhaj
Rām rām bas rām rām bhaj (2x)

He is the cure for all ills. Ram alone is the solution to all problems, glory to Ram. When you are surrounded by problems, O foolish mind, chant the name of Ram.

madhur nahī kōyī gīt rām sā
nikaṭa nahī kōyī mīt rām sā
rām rām jay jay rām rām (2x)
Amṛit madhumayī jīvan chāhē
rām rām ras rōm rōm rach
Rām rām bas rām rām bhaj (2x)

There is no other song as sweet. There is no beloved closer than Ram. Glory to Ram. If you desire a life of sweet ambrosia, let the nectar of the name of Ram arise in every cell.

rām nām bin jñān na kōyī
rām chōḍ vijñān na kōyī
rām rām jay jay rām rām (2x)
Jagatī kē sab bhēd khulengē
rām nām kā karalē jap tap
Rām rām bas rām rām bhaj (2x)

Without the name of Ram there can be no knowledge. Other than Ram there is no experience. Glory to Ram. All of the secrets of creation will be revealed by repeating the name of Ram.

rām kī mahimā yōgī gavē
bhagat rām bhaj rām hī pavē
rām rām jay jay rām rām(2x)
Prabhu kā pāvan mandir ban jā
niś din pal pal rām nām bhaj
Rām rām bas rām rām bhaj (2x)

The glories of Ram are sung by the Yogis. Devotees who chant the name of Ram attain Him, glory to Ram. Transform yourself into the sacred temple of the Lord. Day and night, every moment, chant the name of Ram.

Rām rām bōlō rām rām (2x)
rām rām bas rām rām bhaj
rām rām bas jay jay rām

Chant the name of Ram, worship Him. Victory to Ram.

JVALANA KALYĀṆA

Jvalana kalyāṇa mēghamāy enmanō
gagana vīthiyil nī varū daivamē
kadanamāḷumen vēpathu chētasil
tuhinaśītāśudhārayāy tīraṇē

O Mother, come like a radiant, beneficent cloud through the pathway of the open sky of my mind. Into the sorrowful recesses of my trembling being, come as the cool moonlight.

Vimalamākuken mānasam nirmalē
sajalamākuken nētra tīraṅgaḷe
jvalitamākuken ōrmakaḷ eppozhum
saphalamākuken jīvitam santatam

Make my mind pure, O pure one! May the corners of my eyes shine with tears that arise in longing for You. May my memories of You shine in my mind, O let this life be fulfilled for eternity.

Sakalanēravum nērāṇenikku nī
aṟivinappuṟatt ānandam āṇu nī
akaleyallātma sāramāṇ amma nī
azhivezhātullorāgamakkātal nī

You remain forever my only truth. The inner bliss beyond the intellect is Your real essence. We can never be separate, as You reside in me as my own true Self. You are the indestructible principles of the scriptures.

Eḷimayil nilam pattinin uḷkkaḷam
eriyumāśayonnammay ōṭōtiṭām
iṭaviṭāte nin pādasmaraṇayil
uṇaraṇam amṛtānanda pūrṇamāy

My heart aches for Your grace, it is ablaze to reveal its yearning to You, Mother. In the unrelenting remembrance of Your holy feet, may the full-moon of eternal bliss arise.

JYĀ JYĀ ṬHIKKĀṆI

Jyā jyā ṭhikkāṇi man jhāy mājhē
tyā tyā ṭhikkāṇi nij rūp tujhē
mī ṭhēvitō mastak jyā ṭhikāṇi
tēthē tujhē viṭhalā pāyadōni

Wherever my mind goes, there I see Your divine form. Wherever I put my head, Vithala, Your lotus feet are there.

Viṭhalā viṭhalā viṭhalā viṭhalā
ānanda jhālārē darśanī viṭhalā
prēmānē harṣalā man pāhūna viṭhalā
viṭhalā viṭhalā viṭhalā viṭhalā

From the darshan of Vithala I entered a state of ecstasy. By seeing Him, my mind filled with love and I became blissful.

Amṛtā tsā pān tujhē gōḍnām
tujhē gōḍ chintana ātma sukha dān
mitra tujh gharā jagāt sakalā
sukṛtān chē phal rē bhēṭalā viṭhalā

The repetition of Your sweet name is like a drink of nectar. The contemplation of You gives the bliss of the Self. You are the friend of all beings in the universe. Due to the fruit of my previous good actions I have met You, O Vithala.

Sadā mājhē sanga tujhē divya nām
tujhē gōḍ chintan param pada dān
paramānand rē paramānand
uttam sudin āj bhēṭalā viṭhalā

May Your divine name be always with me. The sweet contemplation of You brings us to the supreme state. O supreme bliss. Today, having seen Vithala, is the best of days.

KADANA BHĀRAM

Kadana bhāram tāñguvān
kazhiyātalayum ēzha ñān
karuṇa nirayum hṛdayamuḷḷoru
viśvam ātāvallē nī (2x)

Helplessly I wander. Due to this burden of grief that I bear I am unable even to sustain myself. Are You not the universal Mother whose heart is filled with compassion?

Abhayam āśichambikē nin
savidham aṇayunninnu ñān
kṛpa tuḷumbum mizhikalālī
yēzhaye nōkkēṇamē (2x)

My desire is to come near to You and seek refuge from You. Please look at me with Your eyes of overflowing compassion.

Varaḷumī marujīvitē mazha -
mēghamāy vannīṭu nī
amṛta peytānanda śītaḷa
dhārayākkiyozhukkiṭū (2x)

Please come as a rain filled cloud into this dry desert of my life. Allow Your nectarine bliss to flow.

Aṇayumō nin padatalēyi
nnente jīvan ambikē
azhalakannamṛtozhukiṭān
ivanilum kṛpa tūkaṇē

O Mother, bring my life close to Your feet; show Your Grace to me. Remove all sorrow and allow Your nectar of bliss to flow towards me.

KĀLIMĀTĒ JAG KĪ MĀTĒ

Kālimātē jag kī mātē
dīnā nāthe jai hō tērī

Victory to Kali, the Mother of the universe and the protector of those who suffer.

Śyāmē śakti śambhu priyē
bhakti pradē dēnā mukti

Dark complexioned one, Shakti, beloved of lord Shiva, one who grants devotion, kindly bestow the final liberation upon me.

Vānīrūpē vidyādātri
vīnālōle gānapriyē

Saraswati, goddess of knowledge, You love music and play upon the veena.

Māyā rūpē, mātē gaurī
sārī sṛṣṭī tērī līlā!

Mother Gauri, Your form is Maya and this entire creation is Your sport.

KALPĀNTARANGALKKUM

Kalpāntarangalkkum appurattākumor-
albhuta ramya svarūpam
albhuta ramya svarūpam
peṭṭennaṭimalar toṭṭuvandi chīṭan
ettukayāṇival ammē ettukayāṇival ammē

I hasten to prostrate at the sacred feet of the Mother of astonishingly beautiful form who transcends the many cycles of time.

Ā ramya harmmyattil āzhān kotipūṇṭu
tēngukayāṇivalennum tēngukayāṇivanennum
nī varumō ente mānasappoykayil
nīnti nīrāṭiṭānammē ennum
nīnti nīrāṭiṭān ammē

I yearn always to dwell in a place made pure, Mother. Won't You come to the still pool of my mind and bathe there?

Ārākilum manam ēkān maṭikkāttor
ālamba śāli tan pādē ālambaśāli tan pādē
ī makalkkum kotiyērunnu dēvi nin
pūjāmalarāy tīrān pūjāmalarāy tīrān

I take refuge at the feet of that exalted one who eases the sorrows of one and all. Goddess, the longing of this child to become a mere flower fit for You to offer in worship is increasing.

KĀṆAKKAṆ KŌṬI

Kāṇakkaṇ kōṭi vēṇṭum
annai kātyāyaniyām
amṛtēśvarī ezhilē ennammā

My dear Mother, immortal goddess, Katyayani, I need a thousand eyes to enjoy Your beauty.

Arul vaṭivam dharitta annaiyai kaṇṭenten
perum piravi eṭutta palanai aṭaintēnē
irul nīkki ulakālum arum perumtattuvattin
porul unarnta bhaktarkal pōtrippukazhttum annai

My birth has become fruitful because I have seen my Mother, the embodiment of compassion. She is the incarnation of the Supreme Principle that rules the whole world and removes darkness. My Mother is praised by those devotees who are knowers of that Truth.

Tellattelivāka tenkōṭi vānatta
veḷḷachuṭaraṭiye pōṇmalar kānti kaṇṭēn
kallam kapaṭamillā piḷḷai mukham kaṇṭēn
ullam niṛainta anpin punnagai pūttukaṇṭēn

My Mother, clad in pure white garments, lit up the skies with a dazzling and golden radiance. When You beheld this innocent child's face, Mother, I felt Your heart overflowing with motherly love, and I saw Your face blossoming into a loving smile.

Abhirāmi valliyām amṛtānandamayi tan
tiruvavatāram seyta maṇ tēṭisentru kaṇṭēn
kaṭal alai pāṭiyāṭa kaṛumukhilōṭi mērkku
kaṭalōratennai kāttil tāṇḍhavan āṭakaṇṭēn

I went in search of the place that is sanctified by the birth of the Divine Mother incarnate, Mata Amritanandamayi. Even the ocean waves in that sacred land dance and sing with joy, and the dark clouds in the western skies swerve happily along with the cool ocean breeze.

KAṆAMUM MAṚAVĒN

Kaṇamum maṛavēn kaṇṇā - unnai
kaṇṇāṛa kāṇbatenṭrō
kaṇṇin oliyāy uyirin uyirāy
kalanta nirkkum kaṇṇā (2x)

O Krishna, I will not forget You even for one instant. You are the life of my life and the light of my eyes. When will my eyes be filled with the sight of You, Krishna?

Ettanai porulkaḷai tantāy
ettanai uravukaḷ aḷittāy
anaittum azhintakantrālum entrum
tuṇayāy iruppatu nīyē (2x)

You have bestowed material objects and numerous relations upon us, Kanna. But all of those things may leave us at any time. You alone will always remain as our firm support.

Aruḷin arumaiyai aṛiyāmal
poruḷin perumaiyai dinam nāṭi
pollā vinai kaḷil āzhāmal - unnil
kalantiṭa vazhi seyvāy kaṇṇā (2x)

Without fully realizing the greatness of Your Grace we have wasted too many days running after the temporal riches of this world. O Kanna, won't You show us the way to forever merge into You? Please guide us away from all of our evil actions.

KANIVU KINIYUMIRU

Kanivu kiniyumiru tēnaruvi
nin mizhi chalamizhi
nīlattāmaradalamizhi
kanivu kiniyumiru tēnaruvi

Your eyes resemble the petals of the blue lotus; never do they remain at rest. They are fountains of sweet compassion.

Śilayil viriyunnorazhakalla nī
viralāl virachikkum kavitayalla
azhalinnulayil uruki teḷiyum
karaḷil nurayunno ranubhūti nī

You are not the beauty that unfolds in a stone sculpture or in a poem written by a human hand. Rather, when the heart has been purified through the fire of the furnace of sorrow, You are the experience of peace that springs up afterwards.

Mahā manasvikal pōlum
mahā tapasvikal pōlum
ninnapadāna kathāmṛta lahariyil
nimagnarākunnū ullam ni śabda mākunnū

Even great souls that have engaged in great austerities become immersed in the intoxication of singing Your praise. Their hearts become still.

Sakala manassilumarivāyuṇarum
nikhila charāchara janani
śritajana hṛdaya sarōruha malaril
amṛtarasānandam janani nijaparamānandam

O Mother of the world, You awaken in every heart as knowledge. You are the nectar of bliss in the hearts of all those who have taken refuge in You. Mother, You are the supreme bliss.

KAṆṆAN ENKĒ

Kaṇṇan enkē kaṇṇan enkē
kaṇkal tēṭutē
unnai kaṇṭa kaṇkal vēru
etaiyum verukkatē

Where is Kannan? My eyes are longing to look at Him. The eyes that have seen Kannan grow tired of looking at anything else.

Uṇṇattantāy uṭuka tantāy
unai marakkavā
ennaittantu iṇaiyaṭi kīzh
enṭrum irukkavā

O Lord, You gave to me all of the comforts of the world. Was that to make me forget You? No, it was to help me surrender myself at Your feet.

Ponnai tandāy porulai tandāy
pukazhil mayakkavā
pūkal chintum un chirippil
ennai izhakkavā

O Lord, You gave me wealth and prosperity. Was all of that just to make me forget myself? No, it was to help me remember Your smiling face. Remembering that face, I forget about everything else.

Gangai tannil kalanda pinnāl
kalankam ērkkavā
gangai unnai ninaittu vāzhkai
kaṭamai ātravā

After one submerges oneself in the Ganges river, can one still have any sins? In the same way, after coming to You, Lord, I should no longer act in a wrong manner. Let me be like the Ganges river that does its duty without expecting anything in return.

Untan kaiyil ennai enṭrō
oppaṭaittiṭṭēn
enna tān vanda pōtum
tāyin poruppenṭrēn

I have surrendered myself to You, Lord. Now it is Your responsibility to take care of me, as a mother takes care of her child, in all of the situations of life.

KAṆṆAN VRAJATHIL

Kaṇṇan vrajathil vaḷarnna kālam
kaṇṇu kaḷkkutsavam āyirunnu
uṇṇi kaḷkkūṇilluṛakkamilla
kaṇṇante kaṇṇāyavar vaḷarnnu

Vraja was a festival before one's eyes when Krishna grew up there. The cowherd boys, lost in their joy, would often forget to eat or sleep. They grew up as darlings of Krishna.

Vātsalyamōṭe vrajāmganakaḷ
vāsaram pārttu pārttaṅgirunnu
pālveṇṇa kaṇṇan kavarnneṭukkān
pākattil vachaṅgoḷiññirunnu

The women of Vraja would await their opportunity to catch a glimpse of Krishna. They would set out butter and milk hoping that Krishna would come to steal them. Then they would wait in hiding for His arrival.

Ōrō manassinṭe pālkkuṭavum
kaṇṇanuṭachu kuṭichirunnu
ōṭakkuzhalocha kēṭṭiṭumbōl
orō manassum trasichirunnu

Their minds were like milk pots; Krishna drank from those pots and then broke them. As they heard His flute their hearts were overcome with joy.

Kōmaḷattariḷam mēni kāṇkē
kōḷmayirkoṇṭu tarichirunnu
bālagōpālanṭe līla kāṇkē
kālam chalikkān marannirunnu

As they beheld His beautiful young body they felt ecstatic, and the hair on their bodies stood on end. Even time became mesmerized by the antics of Krishna and forgot to move forward.

Raṇṭitaḷ tāmara cheṇṭupōle
nīṇṭiṭampeṭṭa mizhiyiṇakaḷ
kaṇṭālakatār niṛaññu kaṇṇil
uṇṭāmanant ānandā srudhāra

His beautiful long eyes looked like lotus petals. Seeing those beautiful eyes in my mind, my eyes became filled with tears of joy.

Rakṣitāvennu chilarariññu
śikṣitāvennu chilarkku tōnni
atbhuta līlakaḷōrttu svantam
arbhakanmāre maṛannirunnu

Some people thought Krishna to be their savior, while others considered Him to be one who may dispense punishment. When they remembered the divine acts of Krishna, they would forget their own infants.

Akkālam kamsan uṛakkamilla
uḷbhayam māṛānu pāyamilla
mṛtyu sānniddhyam maṇattuchuttum
vidvēṣa bhaktyā vimukti nēṭi

Kamsa was often disturbed in his sleep by a fear that he could not allay in any way. He smelt the presence of death about him. Through his constant contempt of Krishna he attained liberation.

Gōkulam gōpālabālanillēl
jīvittuṭippatta dēhamāyi
mṛtyu virōdhiyām kaṇṇanuṇṇi
hṛttilēvarkkum amṛtamāyi

Without Krishna, Gokulam became lifeless. Krishna, who is antagonistic towards death, was like ambrosia in the minds of those who knew Him.

Ambāṭippaitalen pūmanassil
pūttumbiyeppōl parannu vannu
nandanōdyāna sugandhamāyi
antarangattil pataññu ninnu

Krishna, the child of Anbadi, flew through my mind as if He were a butterfly. Like the beautiful fragrance of Nanda's garden, He filled my mind.

Uḷḷile paimbāl kaṭaññiṭumbōḷ
veṇṇapōl pontumī kaṇṇanuṇṇi
chintānabhassil niṛaññutingi
chentāmarākṣan teḷiññu minni

Krishna churns the milk of our mind and He arises as the butter. He with lotus petal eyes, fills the sky of my thoughts and shines bright and clear in my mind.

KAṆṆINDALLADE

Kaṇṇindallade hṛdayada kaṇṇinda
kṛṣṇana nānindu kaṇṭē - enna
rādhā ramaṇanā kaṇṭē - enna
rādhā ramaṇanā kaṇṭē

Today I have seen my dear Krishna, the beloved of Radha. I did not see Him with my external eyes, I saw Him with my inner eye.

Sankalpa chōranā saundarya rūpanā
sangīta gāranā kaṇṭē - enna
sāyūjya nāthanā - enna
sāyūjya nāthanā kaṇṭē

I have seen the one who steals our minds. He is beauty personified. He is the divine musician. I have seen the Lord of eternity.

Nīla kaṭal varṇṇanallavē kṛṣṇā
śiradali navilgari illavē
muraliya gānada nādadolu nā
kōmala rūpanā kaṇṭē

I cannot say if He was the color of the ocean, or if He had a peacock feather adorning His hair. From the sound of His flute I experienced His presence.

KAṆṆINNU PINNILE

Kaṇṇinnu pinnile jyōtiyāy
kāṇāy lōkaṅgaḷ kākkumammē
ammē ammē jagadambikē
lalitāmbā lalitāmbā

By the strength of Your eyes that sparkle with light, Mother, You rule the world. Mother, my darling Mother, Lalitamba.

Mahādēvanuṭe tiru māril chērum
mṛdula manōhara padayugaḷam
lasippatennō ennuṭeyuḷḷil
layippatennō nin chēvaṭiyil

With Your tiny feet, You stand on the chest of the supreme Lord Shiva. My heart aches with longing for the gentle touch of those blessed feet, O Lalitamba.

Samasta dēva ṛṣi muni gaṇaṅgaḷum
sakala charāchara sṛṣṭikaḷum nī
tannuṭe nṛttavilōla padaṅgaḷil
tāyē chērppū nūpura maṇiyāy

The mighty gods, the venerable sages, all of creation itself, all that is alive or still, all of that do You tie onto Your anklets when You dance in bliss, Lalitamba.

Chañchalamasthiram āyikam ulakil
charaṇasarōjam atonnē śaraṇam
aṭiyanumammē nin padakamalam
lalitāmbā lalitāmbā

Your sacred feet are the sole support of this fickle, ever changing universe. I seek refuge at those blessed feet, Lalitamba.

KAR LĒ MĀ KĀ

Kar lē mā kā nit sumiran
arppit karkē tū tan man
chōḍ dē jag kī tū lagan
mā kō basā lē apnē man

Remember Mother always in your mind. Offer your body and mind to Her. Give up your attachment to this world and install Mother in your heart.

Mā mā mā japlē mā mā mā

Chant "ma, ma, ma."

Jab tak hē mē aur mērā
man mē rahēga andhērā
kahnā mā sab hē tērā
hō jāyēgā ujiyārā

As long as the notion of 'I' and 'mine' exists, your mind will be filled with darkness. Say "O Mother, everything is Thine alone!" and the darkness will vanish. The mind will be immersed in the radiant light of grace.

Māyā nē jō ghērā man
chūṭ gayā mā kā bhajan
bīt rahā hē har ēk kṣan
vyartha na hō tērā jīvan

Your mind has been so submerged in delusion that you have forgotten the bliss of singing Mother's name. Every second is slipping away unnoticed – may your life not pass by in vain.

Prēm sē bhaj lē mā kā nām
karnā dil sē tū praṇām
pāyēgā tū mā kā dhām
param śānti kā maṅgala dhām

Sing Mother's name with love and bow down to Her from your heart. Then you will attain Mother's abode, that auspicious abode of supreme peace.

KARUṆĀMAYĪ DĒVĪ (KANNADA)

Karuṇāmayī dēvī kayi mugive
kāruṇyāmṛtava bēḍi kayi mugive
kālannu hiḍiyuva gatigeṭṭa kandage
kāruṇya nīḍu endu kayi mugivē ammā
kāruṇya nīḍu endu kayi mugivē

O compassionate Goddess, we salute You with joined palms. We salute You for the nectar of Your compassion. We prostrate at Your feet that Your compassion may fall on us.

Ajñānagattalalli sikkikoṇṭēvu nāvu
vijñāna dīpa tōru kayimugive
ānandarūpiṇi amṛtēśvari dēvī
kāruṇyāmṛtava bēḍi kayi mugive

We are lost in the darkness of our ignorance. We salute You with joined palms, O blissful, immortal Goddess. We salute You for the light of Your knowledge. We salute You for the nectar of Your compassion.

Karuṇāmayi prēmamayi
amṛtānandamayi kayimugive
kāruṇyāmṛtava bēḍi kayi mugive

Compassionate one, embodiment of love, Mother of immortal bliss, we salute You. We salute You for the nectar of Your compassion.

Kāmādigalā mālinya nīgendu
kāruṇyamūrtti nin aḍigaḷa namipe
prēma svarūpiṇi amṛtēśvari dēvī
kāruṇyāmṛtava bēḍi kayi mugive

We bow down to Your holy feet, incarnation of love and compassion. Immortal Goddess, we bow down to You that You may rid us of impurities such as lust and anger. We salute You for the nectar of Your compassion.

Karuṇāmayi prēmamayi
amṛtānandamayi kayimugive
kāruṇyāmṛtava bēḍi kayimugive

Compassionate one, embodiment of love, Mother of immortal bliss, we salute You. We salute You for the nectar of Your compassion.

KARUNĀMAYĪ DĒVI (TELUGU)

Karunāmayī dēvi ninne kolichēdā
karuṇyāmṛtan kōri ninne kolichēdā
karamule jōṭinchi unnāmu mēmu
kāruṇyāmṛtam kōri ninne kolichēdā - ammā

O divine Mother, You are compassionate. We worship You. With joined palms. We pray to You for the sweet nectar of Your Grace.

Ajñāna kūpamlō munigina mālō
vijñāna velugē chūpincha rāvē
ānanda rūpiṇi hṛdayēśvarī dēvī
kāruṇyāmṛtam kōri ninne kolichēdā

To dispel the darkness of ignorance in which we are drowning, O Mother, please show us the light of knowledge. O blissful one, dwelling in our hearts, we pray to You for Your Grace.

Karuṇāmayi prēmamayi
amṛtānandamayi ninne kolichēdā
kāruṇyamṛtam kōri ninne kolichēdā

O compassionate Mother, Mother of immortal bliss, embodiment of love, we pray to You for Your Grace.

Kāmādulanē mālinyamulanu
kāruṇya mūrtti nī tolagin chavammā
snēha svarūpiṇi hṛdayēśvarī dēvī
kārunyamṛtam kōri ninne kolichēdā

Benevolent Mother, remove from us our lust and our other impurities. O blissful one, dwelling in our hearts, we pray to You for Your Grace.

Karuṇāmayi prēmamayi
amṛtānandamayi ninne kolichēdā
kāruṇyamṛtam kōri ninne kolichēdā

O compassionate Mother, Mother of immortal bliss, embodiment of love, we pray to You for Your Grace.

KĀYĀMBŪNĪLADYUTI

Kāyāmbūnīladyuti minimaññu
kāḷindi tīram iruṭṭilāzhnnu
kārvēṇi rādhayum tōzhimārum
kārkoṇṭamānampōl tēṅgininnu

The blue radiance of the day has faded and Kalindi has sunk into darkness. Lovely Radha and Her friends shed tears as if there were a cloud-laden sky.

Kaṇṇante pūmēniyonntenyē
kāṇuvānāvātta kaṇṇukaḷum
kōṭakkārvarṇṇante nādamonnē
kēḷkkuvān nēdicha kātukaḷum

Those eyes that were unable to see anything but Krishna's beautiful form, those ears that were created only for hearing His beautiful voice,

Kṛṣṇante kinnāram cholluvānāy
kautukam pūṇṭorā nāvumonnāy
kāruṇyarūpane mātramōrttu
karmavum dharmavum viṭṭu māzhki

and those tongues eager to tell His tale, they were all despondent when thinking of that compassionate one and forgetting all else.

Gōpikal andharāy mūkarāyi
kēzhviyum keṭṭavarāyi māṛi
gōpikāṛāṇiyām rādhikaykkō
gōkulam tīcūzhum kānanamāy

The Gopis became blind, mute and deaf in their grief. To Radha, the queen of the Gopis, their cowherd village was now like a forest on fire.

Kuññāyi vannu piṟannatoṭṭē
kālanāy kaṇṭorā kamsanum nī
kanivārnnu kaivalyamēkiyillē
kāliyadarppavināśakanē

O Lord, who crushed the pride of the serpent Kaliya, didn't You grant liberation to that Kamsa who saw You as the lord of death from the moment You were born?

Kāḷindiyāttilinnōḷamillā
vṛndāvanattinō nāthanilla
kaṇṇanekkāttiṭum kālkṣaṇam pōlumē
manvantaraṅgaḷāy māṟiṭunnu

There are no waves in the Yamuna now, Vrindavan has no master. Even a fraction of a second that we spend waiting for Krishna feels like a long, long epoch.

Kaṇṇinnu kaṇṇāyoruṇṇikaṇṇā
kaṇmunnilettānamāntamentē
kaṇṇā nīyettuvān vaikiyennāl
kaṇṇāṇe nin padam pūkum prāṇan

Darling Kanna, You are the apple of my eye, why do You delay to come before me? If You are late in arriving, this soul will leave its body and seek Your holy feet.

Śrī kṛṣṇa gōvinda harē murārē
hē nātha nārāyaṇa vāsudēva

O Krishna, master of the senses and Lord of the universe.

KHUŚIYŌM KĪ BAHĀR

Sarvē bhavantu sukhinaḥ
sarvē santu nirāmayaḥ
sarvē bhadrāṇi paśyantu
mā kaśchid duḥkha bhāgbhavēt

May all beings be happy and without sorrows. May all see only the good that is in everything.

Khuśiyōm kī bahār chaltī rahē
jag mē śānti samāyē rahē
niṣkām nisvārth banē rahē – prabhū
tērī ōr hī baḍ tē rahē

May the spring of joy burst forth. May the world be filled with peace. O Lord, may we become selfless and free of desires and thus may we progress steadily towards You.

Sukhī rahē sabhī jag mē
bhagavān dikhē sab kō sab mē
pyār kī jyōti jalē man mē
jiyē sabhī sadā milan mē

Let all people in the world be content. Let them see the divine spark in all others, and let the light of love shine in their hearts. May all live in harmony.

Mil kē ham pūjē milkē
ham chāhē japē ham sadā
lōkāḥ samastāḥ sukhinō bhavantu – ōm
lōkāḥ samastāḥ sukhinō bhavantu

Let us pray and hope together. We will chant constantly the divine mantra that is a prayer for the entire world to be happy.

KṚPĀ HŌ TĒRI

Kṛpā hō tēri vighnavināśak
kṛpā hō praṇavākār
kṛpā hō dēva gajānanā tērī
kṛpā hō śambhukumār

May You bless us, Lord Ganesha, remover of obstacles, the embodiment of the sound of "OM", the son of Shiva.

Girijā nandana tērī pūjā
pehle karē sab kōyī
vighnavināśan vighnanōm kā tū
kar lē anta kṛpā hō

You are worshipped by all before any other form of God, O son of Parvati. Bless us by removing all of our obstacles.

Mānava dānava dēva munīśvar
karttē tērī pūjā
sab par tū karttā hē jaldi
kṛpā sē mangala varṣā

Humans, deities, saints and sages all worship You. You bless all with an abundance of auspiciousness.

Vidyā budhi vighnaśānti sab
tērē karuṇa phal hē
ham par sadā hō tērī karuṇā
kṛpā hō tēri ham par

When You shower Your compassion on us we are blessed with knowledge and with relief from the obstacles that lay in our path. May Your compassion and blessings always be upon us.

KṚPĀ KARŌ

Har karma mērā hē prabhu
pūjā tērī ban jāyē
kadam baḍē jis rāh par
tujhē milan karāyē

May each of my actions be a pooja to You. May the path that I tread lead me to merge with You

Kṛpā karō ham pē dātā
man yē aur na ḍōlē
mantra jape nitt tyāg kā - sadā
prēm ki bhāṣā bōlē

O Lord, bestow Your grace upon me that this mind does not wander aimlessly. May it always chant the mantra of renunciation. May it always speak the language of love.

Jab jīvan mē khuśiyā āyē
bhūl tujhē na jāyē
dukh āyē jab jīvan mē prabhu
na viśvās uṭṭ jāyē

When life becomes full of happiness, may I not forget You. When sadness comes, may I never lose faith in You.

Jag sē jab ham lēngē vidāyi
pās tujhē hi pāyē
hōṭṭō mē tērā nām rahē - man
tujh mē hī harṣāyē

When I am about to depart from this earth, may I find You near me. May my lips utter Your divine name. May my mind revel in You alone.

KṚPALO KṚṢṆA

Kṛpalo kṛṣṇa kṛpalo kṛṣṇa
rādhā vallabha gōpi jana priya
hē madhusūdana kṛṣṇa (2x)

O compassionate Krishna, dear friend of Radha and the Gopis, You destroyed the demon Madhu.

Karayunnu manas en kaṇṇanil cheruvān
madhurā dhipatiyē tēdi allanzhu ñān
dukha bāram dharichu kṛṣṇa nāmam japichu
kaṇṇane tēdi nadannu ñān ennum kṛṣṇanē tēdi nadannu ñān

My heart is crying to be one with You. I have wandered everywhere in my search for You. I have been sorrowful and called out Your name as I searched for You everyday.

Ni ariyunuvo en viraha dukham kaṇṇa
ī dukha jvalayil ñān niri pidayunnu
manassinu kulirayi bhaktanu tanalaye
darśaṇam kattukille kṛṣṇa (2x)

Do you know the pain that I feel as a result of my separation from You? I feel as if I am burning in a fire. To soothe my heart and comfort me as if I were in shade, please grant to me the vision of You, Krishna.

Andhakāram varunnu ātma prakāṣam tarū
adyanta mūrte nin karunā nī arullu
akitikku gati nīyē adiyannu tuna nīyē
manasil anayukille kṛṣṇa
abhayam chiriyukille

I see darkness all around me; please allow the inner light to dawn within me. O foremost Lord, show me Your compassion. You are my savior and my support. Won't You stay in my heart and grant me refuge, Krishna?

KṚṢṆĀ KANHAIYA

Kṛṣṇā kanhaiya goparipāla
vrajavana kunjavihari murāri
natavara natavara nandakumāra
hē muralidhāra hē giridhāri

O Krishna, protector of the cows, who dwells in the forests of Vraj, destroyer of the demon Mura, O dancer, son of Nanda, You carry a flute and You lifted the Govardhana mountain.

Mujhe darṣan dēdo kṛṣṇā kṛṣṇā
tērē ṣaran mē lēlō kṛṣṇā kṛṣṇā
is dil mē rehna kṛṣṇā kṛṣṇā

Please give me Your darshan (vision of the Lord) Krishna, let me take refuge in You. Krishna, always reside in my heart.

Sukh jāta hai dukh āta
dukh jāta hai sukh āta
par is jīvan mē dukh hi dukh sē
dūb raha he tērē bina

Happiness goes and sorrows come; then sorrows go and happiness comes. But in this life of mine I am drowning in sorrow after sorrow when I am without You.

Rādhe rādhe tu hi jāne
hamre kānha badi natkat hai

dil ki pida tu hi jāne
is natkat ko tu samjhao

O Radha, only You understand that this Krishna of ours is mischievous. You understand the pain that one's heart can feel. Please make Krishna understand.

KṚṢṆA KṚṢṆA JAYA RĀDHĀKṚṢṆA

Kṛṣṇa kṛṣṇa jaya rādhākṛṣṇa
kṛṣṇa kṛṣṇa jaya gōpī kṛṣṇa
kṛṣṇa kṛṣṇa muralī dhara bālā
kṛṣṇa kṛṣṇa manamōhana rūpa

Victory to Krishna who holds the flute and has an enchanting form.

Patmanābha vasudēva tanūjā
vṛṣṇi vamśatilakā vimalāmgā
bhaktavatsala bhayāpaha dēvā
rakṣitākhila jagatrayanāthā

With the lotus blooming from Your navel, adornment on the clan of Vrishnis, You embody purity. You are full of love for Your devotees, You remove all of our fears and You protect the three worlds.

Mandahāsamukha manmatharamyā
sundarāmga sukha kandamukundā
kuñjavāsi munivandyavarēṇyā
śankarādinuta śōbhanarūpā

Adorned with a smiling face and a beautiful body as charming as cupid, the source of happiness for all, You grant liberation.

Rādhikā hṛdaya rājitamūrttē
rāsalōla rasikōttama śaurē
vēṇugānarasa līna murārē
vēda vēdya viditākhila viṣṇō

You adorn the heart of Radha and You enjoy the dance of the Gopis. Descendent of Shurasena, absorbed in the music of the flute, slayer of Mura, knower of the Veda, You are omniscient.

MĀ AMṚTĒŚVARI

Mā amṛtēśvari maṅgala dāyini mā
jaya jagadhō dhāriṇi jaya jaga jananī mā
mā amṛtēśvari (3x) mā

Mother, the Immortal Goddess who showers auspiciousness upon us, victory to You who uplift the whole universe.

Bhakti dijō mā prēma dijō mā
darṣan dijō mā kṛpā karō mā
mā amṛtēśvari (3x) mā

Please grant us devotion, please grant us love, please bestow upon us the vision of You. Shower Your grace on us, O Mother, Immortal Goddess.

Prēma svarūpiṇi mā tripura sūndari mā
sarvalōka jananī mā jaya jaga jananī mā
mā amṛtēśvari (3x) mā

Embodiment of love, beautiful one, Mother of all the worlds, victory to the universal Mother, the immortal Goddess!

MAHITA SNĒHA MAHĀRṆṆAVAM

Mahita snēha mahārṇṇavam - mahārṇṇavam
sukhadādhāra sudhārṇṇavam - amba
mahita snēha mahārṇṇavam

Mother, You are the ocean of supreme love. You are the ocean of nectar that is the basis of lasting joy.

Sakala jīvana dhāra nī - pada
saphalatakku sahāyi nī
hṛdayakamala nivāsini - swara
madhurimaykkamṛtābdhi nī

Mother, You are the current of life that enlivens all beings. You help us to reach the supreme goal. You reside in the lotus of our hearts. You are the nectarine ocean of beautiful music.

Anu padānupadaṅgalāl mana
talirilezhutiya kavita nī
anubhavānta rasāmṛtam - hṛdi
atula saundarya lahari nī.

You are a poem inscribed on the tender leaves of our hearts. You are the eternal sweetness at the end of direct spiritual experience. Mother, You are the incomparable inundation of beauty.

MALAMUKALIL OḶIVITARUM

Malamukalil oḷivitarum
kaliyuga daivam
akamalaril prabha choriyun -
natulita satyam

The God of the Kali Yuga (Ayyappa) spreads His light from His mountaintop. From the flower of the heart, He emits the radiance of the incomparable Truth.

Kanaleriyum manasinavan
amṛtasuvarṣam
tirunaṭayil tozhutuvarum
aṭiyanu harṣam

For the mind that is burning in sorrow, He is a shower of nectar. One who bows at His lotus feet is filled with elation.

Makaradīpam anavaratam
matiyiludikkān
kaniyuka nī viriyaṇamen
hṛdaya pankajam

Be pleased and come and fill the lotus of my heart. Then the divine lights of Sabarimala will forever illumine my intellect.

Manamuruki svamiye yenno –
nnu viḷichāl
anunimiṣam nalkumavan
asulabhaśānti

If one's heart melts as one calls out, "Swamiye!" then one is granted forevermore a peace that is hard to attain.

Śaraṇam ayyappā svāmi śaraṇam ayyappā
svāmi tintakattōm hari hara nandana tintakattōm

I take refuge in Ayyappa. May He grant me His protection and grace.

MANASSENNA MALARVAḶḶIKKULA

Manassenna malarvaḷḷikkula viriññu
samastavum mannasil ninnudicchuyarnnu
madhuvillā malarennatariññiṭāte
madhuvuṇṇāniraṅgiya madhu bhṛmgam ñān

My mind has blossomed as a bouquet of flowers. All things are born from the mind. I am a bee that set out to drink honey, but in those flowers I found no honey.

Jagadamba varumennuṛacchirunnu - enne
ī janamellām mattanāṇennuṛacchu
japamenten aṛiyāte mūkanāy ā -
jananīyettanne ninacchirunnu

I have waited a long time, believing that the Mother of the universe will appear before me. The whole world believes me to be crazy. I don't know how to chant the divine name; I sit silently and think of the divine Mother.

Niravadhi nimiṣaṅgaḷ varṣaṅgaḷāy
nirupicha nidhiyettiṭāte kēṇu
nilatetti alayunna manassinnu nī
nirupamē teḷivēkīṭān varumō

Minutes have turned into years. Not having found the treasure that I have searched for, I weep. O peerless Mother, won't You come and shed some of Your light into this mind that has lost its way and is wandering?

MĀNGU MĒ

Māngu mē tujhsē mā
tum hō varadāyini
kab hōṅgē darśan tērē
tarsē nayanā mērē

O Mother, granter of boons, may I ask from You when will I have Your darshan? My eyes are thirsting to see You.

Kēhatē hē tumkō mā
sadya prasādini
mēri yē vinati kyō mā
kartti hō ansuni
Pānā hē tujhkō mā
kōyi ōr chāh nahi
mā ō mā pukārē jāyē yē tēri santān
svīkārō hṛdayānjali hē amṛtēśvari mā

Mother, aren't You the compassionate one who is extolled in the scriptures as the Mother who readily bestows boons. Then why is the prayer of this child not heard by You? There is no other desire than to seek for You, Mother. Your children are crying for You, O immortal Goddess. Please accept us.

Rahkar bhī itnē pās
mē tumsē dūr kahī
kaisīyē tērī līlā
dēkhā tujh kō nahī
Khēlō na ōr mujhsē
lēlō nij āchal mē
mā ō mā pukārē jāyē yē tēri santān
svīkārō hṛdayānjali hē amṛtēśvari mā

Even though You are so close to us, I am so far away from You. Mysterious is Your divine play, that I have not yet had Your darshan. Please do not play hide and seek with me anymore. Mother, take me in Your arms. Your children are crying for You, O Immortal Goddess, please accept us.

MAN RĒ

Man rē sīkh prabhu kā hōnā
nain mē uma ē gangā jal sē
prabhu charaṇan nit dhōnā
man rē sīkh

O mind, learn to become the Lord's own. With the water of the Ganges river that emerges from your eyes, ever wash the feet of the Lord.

Jitanē viṣayō kō apanāyā
ēk bhī tērē kām na āyā
jis jis kō tu bhī mītā samjhā
us us nē taḍ pāyā
sanchay kar kar umar ga vāyā
sīkh sabhī kuch khōnā
man rē sīkh

Out of the objects of desire that you have experienced, not one has been of any lasting value to you. Whoever you considered as your beloved, that person has caused you pain. Accumulating material possessions for enjoyment, you have wasted your life. Now learn to lose all, O mind.

Bōjh banī hai abhilāṣā yē
khīnch rahī dukh kī rēkhā yē
tū par vaś hō kar kyō rōyā
bāndhī svayam sīmā yē
mukti kahān jō tū nahīn rōkē
bīj karam kā bōnā
man rē sīkh

Desires have now become a burden to you; they create situations of grief. Why do you cry now that you are enslaved? It is you who created your own enslavement. Until you stop planting the seeds of future problems with your current selfish actions, how will you attain to the ultimate state of freedom, O mind?

Jagatī kā har kāraj us kā
har kāraj mē dhyān bhī us kā
khud hī banā yē khud hī miṭā yē
dēś kāl sab us kā
tan kā har kṣaṇ saral samādhī
kyā jag nā kyā sōnā
man rē sīkh

All actions in this world are done by the Lord. In all work it is He alone who creates and destroys. Time and space belong to Him. When such knowledge is gained then in every second of this life we will have awareness of the Truth. Where is sleep or wakefulness in that state, O mind?

MANVĀ RĒ TŪ

Manvā rē tū jāg jāg
nis din gayē bīt rē

O mind! Awake! Arise! The days and nights are passing by.

Chār diśā mat bhaṭak rē
chēn na pāyē sansār mē
ānand sahaj pāyēgā rē
hari charaṇ kē prīt mē (2x)

Do not wander in all directions, O mind. You will not find peace in the world. It is only at the feet of the supreme Lord Hari that you will find everlasting happiness.

Mīt na kōyī is jag mē
prīt na kōyī sansār mē
mīt tū sachā pāyēgā rē
hari charaṇ kē prīt mē (2x)

You have no real relatives in this world, nor are there any that you can truly consider as beloved. Only at the feet of Hari will you find the true beloved of your soul.

Mūrat sē mandir sajē
jyōt sē andhiyārā ṭalē
man kā mēl dhul jāyē rē
hari charaṇ kē prīt mē (2x)

A temple is adorned with an idol. Light is necessary to dispel darkness. At the blessed feet of Hari all of the impurities of the mind are washed away.

MĀTṚ VĀTSALYAM NIRAÑÑU

Mātṛ vātsalyam niraññu tulumbunna
chēṇuta nin susmitānanattin
kāntikkatirente kāntāra chētassil
chintumānanda matulyam ammē

O Mother, the beaming smile on Your face, overflowing with motherly affection, spreads unequalled joy in the forest of my mind.

Prēma sārāmṛta mōlum mizhikaḷenn
ātma hṛdantam tazhukinannāy
śōdhichuṇarttunna harnniśam samsāra
śāntukku pākamākkunnu mēnmēl

Your eyes, filled with the nectar of love, caress and awaken my heart and thus render it fit to gain release from the sorrow of samsara.

Śōkavraṇitamām hṛttil puraṭṭunnu
snēhāmṛtauṣadham nī mahēṣī
kāruṇyamūrttiyennamma – tiruvaḷḷi
kāvil viḷaṅgum jagajananī

O compassionate Mother of the universe, residing in Vallickavu (the village near Amma's ashram in India), You apply the medicine of immortal love to the to the grief-filled wounds in my heart.

Mōhāndhakārattil nērvazhiyōrāte
kāliṭaṛunniḷam paitaṅgaḷil
bhāvipratīkṣatan neyttiriyālazha lātunna
lōkaika nāthē tozhām

Salutations to You, universal Mother, who light the lamp of hope for the future for Your children. We are faltering, having lost our way in the dense darkness of this delusional world.

MAYIL TŌGAI

Mayil tōgai virittādum malar mukhamō
manakōyil vīṭṭirukkum tiru mukhamō
aṭiyavarai kākkum arul mukhamō
amṛtēśvari un divya mukham

Immortal Goddess, is Your divine face like the full spread of a peacock's feathers? Or is it Your face that resides in the temple of my heart? Is it the graceful face that protects the devotees of God?

Naṭuil oli chintum muzhu matiyō
pālai vana naṭuvil oru śōlai vanamō
pārvayāl nōy tīrkkum nal marundō
amṛtēśvari un divya mukham

Immortal Goddess, is it Your divine face, resembling the morning star, that beautifies the sky? Or is it the full moon shining at midnight? Is it the oasis in the middle of the hot desert? Is it that magic cure that can remove all diseases?

Amudamena pāl surakkum tāy mukhamō
ariyāda kuzhantai pōl sēy mukhamō
guruvāgi bhōdikkum jñāna mukhamō
aruvāgum adhai uṇarttum mōna mukhamō
amṛtēśvari un divya mukham

Immortal Goddess, is it Your divine face that reminds one of a loving mother showering ambrosia on her children? Is it the face of an innocent child? Is Your face that of a Guru teaching the supreme knowledge? Perhaps it is that face that makes one experience the attributeless supreme Truth.

MĒ KHADĪ

Mē khadī udī kā rāh
mērē ghar śyām āvēgā
jē śyām nā āyā kōyī pē gām āvēgā

I am standing and waiting for Shyam hoping that he will come to my home. If Shyam will not come, surely he will send a message.

Mē puchā ud dē pamchiyā nu
patā śyām dā
mē ud na sakā āp
khabrā kōn layā vēgā (2x)
jē śyām nā āyā kōyī pē gām āvēgā

I ask the birds that fly overhead if they know where is Shyam. As I am unable to fly myself then who will bring news of me to Shyam? If Shyam will not come, surely he will send a message.

Mē baiṭhī rastā rōk menu
lōkī puch dē
kī lā layā ē rōg tērē
hatt kī āvēgā
jē śyām nā āyā kōyī pē gām āvēgā

I sit disconsolately and others ask me, "What have you done to yourself? What do you hope to gain?" If Shyam will not come, surely he will send a message.

Mē jāgā sārī rāt menu
nīnd na āvē
kad hōvēgī parbhāt
śyām mērā bhērā pavegā (2x)
jē śyām nā āyā kōyī pēgām āvēgā

I stay awake all night unable to sleep. I wonder when the dawn will come and Shyam will arrive. If Shyam will not come, surely he will send a message.

Hun ājā nandalāl mērā
dēkh hāl vē
tērī dāsī dī nayyā pār
kōn lagavēgā
jē śyām nā āyā kōyī pēgām āvēgā

O Nandalal, please come and see my condition. Who is going to take care of this servant of Yours? If Shyam will not come, surely he will send a message.

MĒRĒ VICH RĀM

Mērē vich rām tērē vich rām
sab vich rām samāyā
sabanū karlō prēm jagat vich
kōyī nahī parāyā jī kōyī nahī parāyā

Ram is within me and you; Ram is within everyone. Love all the beings in this world. No one is a stranger.

Khojyā jag sārā mēnnu
kadī rām nahī labyā
hōyī jadō ōdī kṛipā
rām hī rām milyā mēnnu
rām hī rām milyā

I searched across the face of this Earth but I was unable to find Ram. Yet when I was blessed with His grace I then saw Him everywhere.

Sōndayā vēkhū jāgdayā vēkhū
rām hī rām disyā
sapnyā vich vī mēnnu pyārē
dars rām dā milyā mēnnu
dars rām dā milyā

Whether asleep or awake I see Ram. Dear one, in my dreams I see Ram. I have been blessed with the vision of Ram.

Pahāḍā nadiyā bādal vich
rām hī rām vasyā
phullā vich chip chip kar mērē
rām nē mēnnu sadyā
mērē rām nē mēnnu sadyā

Ram dwells in the mountains, the rivers and the clouds. Ram is in the flowers. He beckons to me. Ram beckons to me.

MERISE KANNULA

Merise kannula śaktula to
jagamunu de tallivani
amma na baṅkaramma
lalitāmbā lalitāmbā

By the strength of Your eyes that sparkle with light, Mother, You rule the world. Mother, my darling Mother, Lalitamba.

Parameśwaru ni hṛdayamu pai nī
chinni pādamē petti nilchitivi
ā mṛdu pāda sparśa kōsame
ātura padane nā hṛdayamu

With Your tiny feet, You stand on the chest of the supreme Lord Shiva. My heart aches with longing for the gentle touch of those blessed feet, O Lalitamba.

Dēva dēvulu ṛṣī lantaru
sṛiṣṭi samastamu nī padamulakē
antelu ayī ānanda nṛtyamu
chēsitivē lalitāmbā

The mighty gods, the venerable sages, all of creation itself, all that is alive or still, all of that do You tie onto Your anklets when You dance in bliss, Lalitamba.

Chañchala asthira māyā jagamulō
nī charananulē ēkā dhāramu
nī pādamulanē śaranai nammiti
lalitāmbā lalitāmbā

Your sacred feet are the sole support of this fickle, ever changing universe. I seek refuge at those blessed feet, Lalitamba.

MĒRĪ SUNLĒ ARAJ

Mērī sunlē araj mērī sunlē araj
mērī sunlē arajiyā pyārē śyām
āyē śyām pyārē śyām mērē śyām

Dear Shyam, listen to my plea.

Jamunā taṭ par tū nā āyē
viraha kī agana mē jaltē jāyē
rādhā gōpī vraj jan sārē
ō kānhā mērē kānhā

After all this time You still have not come to the banks of the Yamuna river. Radha, the Gopis and all the other people of Vrindavan burn in the fire of separation, O Krishna.

Rēn yē bītē chēn na āyē
nayana barsē badrā chāyē
ab tō āvō līlādhām rē
ō kānhā mērē kānhā

The night is going by and yet we know no peace. Our eyes rain tears and the clouds cover the sky. Now is the time for You to come at last, lord of the divine play.

Chānd sitārē bhūpar āyē
brahmādika muni sab harśāyē
muralī bajānē ō
muralī bajānē kānhā āyē
rās rachānē kānhā āyē
kānhā āyē rē kānhā āyē

The moon and the stars have descended to the earth. Lord Brahma and the sages all rejoice. Lord Krishna has come to play His flute and to dance.

Rās rachānē kānhā āyē
dhūm machānē kānhā āyē
murali bajānē kānhā āyē
ranga jamānē kānhā āyē

Lord Krishna has come to dance and to celebrate. Lord Krishna has come to play divine melodies on the flute and to fill the world with color.

MINUGUVA KAṆṆINA

Minuguva kaṇṇina śaktiyali
jagavanu āluva tāyiyu nīnē
ammā nanna nalumeya ammā
lalitāmbā lalitāmbā

By the strength of Your eyes that sparkle with light, Mother, You rule the world. Mother, my darling Mother, Lalitamba.

Paramadēvana śivana edeyanu
puṭṭapādadali meṭṭi nintihe
ninnaya pādasparśanakāgi
āturavāgide nannī hṛdaya
lalitāmbā lalitāmbā

With Your tiny feet, You stand on the chest of the supreme Lord Shiva. My heart aches with longing for the gentle touch of those blessed feet, O Lalitamba.

Dēva dēvaru ṛṣi samastaru
sṛṣṭiya nānacharāchara elleva
ninnaya pādasaradali jōḍisi
naliyuve nīnu lalitāmbā
lalitāmbā lalitāmbā

The mighty gods, the venerable sages, all of creation itself, all that is alive or still, all of that do You tie onto Your anklets when You dance in bliss, Lalitamba.

Chañchala asthira māyājagadi
ninna charaṇavē ēkādhāra
ninna pādake śaraṇu bandihe
lalitāmbā lalitāmbā

Your sacred feet are the sole support of this fickle, ever changing universe. I seek refuge at those blessed feet, Lalitamba.

MŌRA MUKUṬA VĀLĒ

Mōra mukuṭa vālē kānhā chitt chōr
rūpa salōnā khīchē tērī ōr
kāhē kō satāyē rē kāhē kō rulāyē
chandā sā mukha ḍā yād dē jā yē

You who wear the crown of peacock feathers, You steal our hearts. Your beautiful form draws us to You. Why do You tease us, why do You make us cry? Your face that resembles the moon cannot be forgotten.

Gajrārē ānkhē vō khumg rālē bāl
vō chōṭṭī chōṭṭī bayyā vō matvālī chāl
jī lal chāyē vō karē burā hāl
yaśōmati mayyā vō nandā kā lāl

Your beautiful eyes are lined with kol and Your hair is curly. Your arms are dainty and You walk in a swinging manner. The desire in my heart to be near You is causing me anguish. O son of Nanda, Yashoda is Your mother.

Tērē liyē mākhana misrī dūdh dahi
hamsē hō rūṭhē kyā yē he sahī
aisē niṣṭhur ban baiṭhē aisē nirmmōhī
tērē bin yē jīvan mē artha hī nahī

We offer You butter, sugar and yogurt. Are You upset with us? Is that fair? How can You become so un-caring and un-loving? There is no meaning in life without You.

MUDDU KṚṢṆĀ

Kṛṣṇā kṛṣṇā ammā hāduvaḷu
malagu – muddu kṛṣṇā

My dear Krishna, mother will sing You a lullaby; please sleep!

Muddu kṛṣṇā nanna muddu kṛṣṇā
puṭṭa kṛṣṇā nanna tuṇta kṛṣṇā
puṭṭa puṭṭa nayanagaḷige nidde bandide nī
malagu kṛṣṇā bēga malagu kṛṣṇā

O darling, innocent Krishna, sleep has come to Your small eyes. Go to sleep soon.

Dinavella ōḍuta nī āḍide krṣṇā
īga puṭṭa pāda heḷide malagū krṣṇā
dinavella muraḷiyannu ūḍide krṣṇā
īga putta nayanagaḷige nidde bandide krṣṇā

All day long You ran and played but now Your baby feet are telling You to go to sleep. All day long You caressed Your flute and now Your baby hands are saying that You should fall asleep.

Dinavella janara manava kadde krṣṇā
īga puṭṭa kangaḷēḷive malagū krṣṇā
jagavannu nagisi nagisi kuṇiside krṣṇā
īga puṭṭa tuṭigaḷeḷive malagū krṣṇā

All day long You stole our hearts; now those innocent eyes say that You should sleep, Krishna! All day long You entertained the world with Your laughter, but now those baby lips are saying to fall asleep.

Kārmōda villi sērive krṣṇā nōḍu
avugaḷū jō jō hāḍive krṣṇā
yamuneyā alegaḷu hāḍive krṣṇā
jaḷa jaḷa jaḷa alegaḷa lāli krṣṇā

The dark clouds have slowly gathered in the sky, Krishna! Even they are singing lullabies to You. The waves of the Yamuna sing to the lapping, gentle lullaby of the river.

Hūvanada sugandhavu sūside krṣṇā
ninna muttive krṣṇā nī malagu krṣṇā
vāyuraja uyyāle tūgiha krṣṇā
nī malagu krṣṇā bēga malagu krṣṇā

The flowers from the garden have exhilarated You, Krishna! The wind has come to rock You to sleep; please sleep soon.

Yasō ammana kandā nadagōpana bālā
jo jo hādide jagavella ninage
jo jo lāli jo jo, lāli lāli jo jo
jagannātha nī malagu begane

Darling of Yashoda and Nanda, the whole world is singing a lullaby to You. O protector of the entire world, please sleep soon.

MUKHI ASUDĒ

Mukhi asudē prabhuchē nām
rām rām jay rājā rām
prēm bhakti dēyi tē nām
rām rām jay rājā rām

Always chant the name of Lord Ram. Repeating that divine name bestows supreme devotion.

Prabhuchē jithē smaraṇa nāhi
dukhtyā manāchē jhāvē nāhi
rām nām japē vinārē
śānti kōṇi pāvē nāhi

Sorrows will remain if we fail to chant the name of God. Without repeating the name of Lord Ram, no one will attain peace of mind.

Sthāna prabhūlā dē mani
dhyān asūdē śrī charaṇi
tujhyā samgē antim kṣaṇi
prabhu vinārē nāhi kōṇi

In our mind, we must reserve a space for the Lord. Let us always contemplate the Lord's holy feet. At our last breath, only the Lord will remain with us.

MUVVALU KATTI

Muvvalu katti ādi ādi ra ra
na chinnari kanna ra tvaraga ra ra
nī chinni pādam vetukutunnamu
nī divya nāmam pāḍutannāmu

O Krishna, endowed with lotus shaped eyes, tie on Your anklets and come running and dancing. Searching for Your tender feet we have come singing the divine names.

Dēvakī nandana rādhā jīvana
kēśavā hare mādhavā
pūtana marddana pāpa vināśana
kēśavā hare mādhavā
gōkula bālane ādi ra ra
gōpāla bālane pādi ra ra

Devaki's son, the very life of Radha, Hare, Madhava, slayer of Putana, destroyer of sins, child of Gokula, cowherd boy, come running and dancing.

Kamsa vimarddana kāliya narttana
kēśavā hare mādhavā
āśrita vatsala āpat bāndhavā
kēśavā hare mādhavā
ōmkāra nādamē ādi ra ra
ānanda gītamē pādi ra ra

Slayer of Kamsa, the dancer upon the serpent Kaliya's head, Kesava, Hare, Madhava, You are affectionate to Your devotees. You protect those in danger, O embodiment of "OM." Come running and dancing.

Pāṇdava rakṣaka pāpavināśana
kēśavā hare mādhavā
arjjuna rakṣaka ajñāna nāśakā
kēśavā hare mādhavā
gītāmṛtamē ādi ra ra
hṛdayānandamē pādi ra ra

Protector of the Pandavas, destroyer of sins, Keshava, Hare, Madhava, O protector of Arjuna, destroyer of ignorance, You are the nectar of the Gita. Bliss of the heart, come running and dancing.

NILAIYILLĀ ULAKIL

Nilaiyillā ulakil nimmati – tēṭi
nittamum nī alaindāy manitā
nimalanaṭi maṛandāy

O man, you are constantly wandering through this impermanent world in search of peace. Alas, you have forgotten the lotus feet of the Lord.

Nāṭāṇṭa mannaṛenkē
nidhiyāṇṭa selvaṛenkē
ēṭāṇṭa pulavaṛenkē
ellōrum pōnatenkē

Where are the mighty kings who ruled the country? Where are those prosperous rulers of wealth? Where are those famous poets who ruled over the kingdom of verse? Where did all these people go?

Matravarai kurai kūṛi
matippatra kālattai
māykkinṭra ivāzhvilē
un kuraiyai arindu nī mati telintiṭṭē

manattūy mayai peru manitā

Instead of killing priceless time by finding fault with others, spend this precious life, O man, in becoming aware of your own shortcomings. Thus with a clear mind find the eternal Truth.

Eppōruḷum enatalla
en uṇmai arindiṭinum
eṇṇatra bandankal ēnō
utra tuṇai avananṭri avaniyil āruḷar
uṇarndu nī śaraṇ puku manitā

Even though we know that nothing is ours, why do we have these innumerable bonds? Realizing that there is no other firm support in this world than the Lord, O man, seek refuge at His holy feet.

NĪLĀMBUJA NAYANĒ (KANNADA)

Nīlāmbuja nayanē ammā
nī naṛiyē ī nōvina chittada aḷalugaḷa
yāvudō janmada lesagida karmmadi
ēkāmgiyāgi nā alediruvē

O Mother, endowed with beautiful blue lotus eyes, are You aware of the misery in this grieving heart? Perhaps it is due to wrong actions that I did in a previous incarnation that I now wander all alone.

Yuga yuga yuga dali janmisi nānī
yuga sandhi yali silukiṛuve
appuveyō muddu gareyuveyō
ninnaya maṭilali irisuveyō ammā

After drifting through several ages of this creation, I have taken birth at the present time. Won't You take me close to You with a motherly hug and place me on Your lap?

Yōgyanallaventu tāyiyu putranā
tyāgamāṭuvalē yōgadhātri
baruveyā nī baḷi kareyuveyā nī
nina kṛpe lavalēśa koṭuveyā nī ammā

O Mother, will You forsake me because I am unworthy of You? Won't You come before me, hold me close to You and bestow Your grace upon me, Mother?

NĪLĀMBUJA NAYANĒ (TELUGU)

Nīlāmbuja nayanē ammā telisēnō lēdō
nā ī chitta śōkamulu
ēdō janmalō chēsina karmamē
ēkāntanai nē tirigēnu

O Mother, endowed with beautiful blue lotus eyes, are You aware of the misery in this grieving heart? Perhaps it is due to the wrong actions that I did in a previous incarnation that I now wander all alone.

Yugāntarālalō tēli tēli ne
ī yuga sandhyalō chēritinē
seda tīrttuvō nannu pālintuvō
nī oḍilō nannē lālintuvō

After drifting through several ages of this creation, I have taken birth at the present time. Will You provide solace for this weary soul? Will You protect me? Will You place me on Your lap and comfort me?

Yōgyata lēdani mātā ī putra ṇī
paritya jintuvō yōgadhātri
rāvēmī dari chēravēmī
nī kṛpā lēsam chūpavēmi ammā
nī kṛpā lēsam chūpavēmī

O Mother, will You forsake me because I am unworthy of You? Won't You come before me, hold me close to You and bestow Your grace upon me, Mother?

NĪRĀJANAM

Nīrājanam nīrājanam
mā talli rūpunaku nīrājanam nīrājanam

I offer Arati (a form of worship) to my Mother's form.

Punnamī rātrilō chandrunila śōbhiñche
mā talli boṭṭunaku nīrājanam
chīkaṭilō dāri chūpi nayiñche
mā talli nattukaku nīrājanam

I offer Arati to our Mother whose sandalwood mark on the forehead is like the moon on the full moon night. I offer Arati to our Mother whose radiant nose ring illuminates our path that is covered in darkness.

Manṭe manassunu challāṛa jēse
mā talli navunaku nīrājanam
tarim pajēsē divya prēmatō ninṭina
mā talli kaṇṇulaku nīrājanam

I offer Arati to our Mother whose laugh cools the burning in out hearts. I offer Arati to our Mother whose eyes uplift us and fill us with divine love.

Ajñānapū andhakārāṇṇi tolagiñche
mā talli palukulaku nīrājanam
pasivāriga mammu pālinchi lāliñchi
mā talli karamulaku nīrājanam

I offer Arati to our Mother whose words drive away the darkness of our ignorance. I offer Arati to our Mother whose hands caress and console us as Her own children.

Parama padāniki paryāyamaina
mā talli padamulaku nīrājanam
alasi solasina ī jivikī nī
pādamula chentane choṭṭunivu

I offer Arati to our Mother whose feet lead us to the ultimate goal. Mother, provide refuge at Your feet for this tired soul.

NIŚAYUṬE NĪRAVA

Niśayuṭe nīrava nīlimayil
nirayum chārum nilāvoliyil
yamunānadiyuṭe tīrattil
yadunāyakanuṭe varavāyi varavāyi

In the deep silence of a blue night illumined with sparkling moonlight, the Lord of the Yadus, Krishna, came to the banks of the Yamuna river.

Mazha mukilazhakezhum uṭalāṇṭōn
mayilin pīlikal aṇiyunnōn
mṛdu malayānilan ozhukumbōl
madhuram vitarān kanivāyi kanivāyi

The soft, cool breeze from the mountains blew gently. He with an enchanting body the color of dark rain clouds and with a peacock feather in His hair came gently to shower His sweetness on all. Gently He came.

Muralikay adharam aṇaññallō
viralukal kuzhalil amarnnallō
mizhiyiṇa mṛdulam aṭaññallō
mōhana gānam utirnnallō utirnnallō

Raising His flute to His lips and placing His fingers on the holes, with his eyes half shut, a haunting melody flowed forth. It flowed forth.

Gōkulamākey ulaññallō
gōpikal mōhitarāyallō
toṭukuri pūkkal aṇiññuṭanē
yamunāpulinam aṇaññallō aṇaññallō

All of Gokula became entranced by that soulful tune. The gopis were lost in love for the flute player. They quickly adorned themselves with flowers and vermillion and sought the banks of the Yamuna river.

Gōpīlāsyalayam paṭarum
muralīgāna taramgiṇiyil
jīvēṣvara milanāvasarē
rāsōtsava sudha cheyunnu sudha cheyunnu

As they were swept away on the waves of the melody of the flute, the gopis began their gentle dance. In that moment their hearts merged with the Lord, the individual soul eternally one with the Supreme Self, and they danced the rasa dance.

Ō MĀ YĒ

Ō mā yē sach hē ki tu sadā sāth hamāra
magar mā afsos yē hē ki itnē karib hotē huyē bhi
kitnē dūr mehasūs karta hūm hum

Mother, though it is the truth that You are always with me, this soul is so ignorant that even while in Your lap I still feel worlds away.

Pal mē mā tū nē itna pyar dīyā jo
sāra jīvan ko savāre
phir bhi yē māṇ bhatakta
hē pyar basanē

In one second You give me enough love to last a lifetime. Yet this soul wanders off longing to be loved.

Mā mujhē māf kārna kyonki bīnā
soche samjhē tujhsē mein
sadā māngtha rahā chudha dō mā mujhē
is jūthi kuṣi ki fisul khōj sē

Please forgive me Mother, for everything that You give me is taken for granted. Please free me from this never-ending search for false contentment.

Mā mērē rakṣa kārna aur mēra har
ṣubdha tēra gun gāye
mēra har dhadkhan tēra pyar sē bharē
mēra har sas sēva kīlaye jage

Cast away my ignorance so that every sound from this tongue is of Your glories, every thought in this mind is born out of love for You and every step of this body is one taken in Your service.

Ō MĒRI PYĀRĪ MAYYĀ

Ō mēri pyārī mayyā
mērī pyāri mayyā mērī dēvī mayyā

ō mēri pyāri mayyā mērī dēvī mayyā

O my dear Divine Mother.

Tū mujh par kar karuṇā tērē
man mēm dayā hō maiyā
pyār se apnā lēnā
ō mērī dēvī mayyā
tēri karuṇā hī ēk sahārā
ō mērī pyārī mayyā

Show me Your compassion and Your love. Your mercy is my only support, dear Mother.

Pyāri mayyā dēvī mayyā pyāri mayyā dēvī mayyā
pyāri mayyā (2x)
ō mērī dēvī mayyā ō mērī pyārī mayyā

O my dear Divine Mother.

Prēm se rakṣa karnā tū
mēre bandana sab dūr karnā
dukhī hē man mērā
ō mērī dēvī mayyā
mujhē śānti kā var dēnā
ō mērī pyārī mayyā

Protect me in Your loving manner, Mother; remove my bondage. I am sad, please bless me with peace.

Tērī gōd mē lēnā mā
mujhkō charaṇ mē āśray dēnā
mērā tū hī ēk sahārā
ō mērī dēvī mayyā
mujhē bhūl na jānā mā
ō mērī pyārī mayyā

Take me in Your arms, Mother; grant me shelter at Your feet. You are my only support, never forget me!

ŌMKĀRA PAÑJARA ŚUKĪM

Omkāra pañjara śukīm
upaniṣadōdyāna kēli kālakaṇṭhīm
āgama vipina mayūrīm āryām
antar vibhāvayēt gaurīm

May I meditate on the Goddess Gauri, the peacock in the forest of the sacred Scriptures. She is like the bird sporting in the cage of the primordial sound, "OM." She plays in the garden of the Upanishads.

Īśvarī ninnē nammiti
lōkaika jananī jagadīśvari – amma

Goddess, Mother of the universe, I have taken refuge in You.

Sanmārggamulanē chupinchi nīvu
sāvitri vaitivammā
gamyamunakē chērchi nīvu
gāyatri vaitivammā

You are Savitri, the one who shows us all the good paths to follow. You are Gayatri, She who leads us to the goal.

Bhakta janmulanu kāppāṭutunna
bhavapatni vaitivammā
kāmmulanē hariñchi nīvu
ā kali vaitivammā

As Parvati You rescue Your devotees. As Kali You remove all of our desires.

Vidvān suni manasū nandu
śrī vidya vaitivammā

bhāgyamulanē onaguchunna
mā bhāgya lakṣmi vammā

You are that exalted knowledge which resides in the hearts of poets. O Bhagya Lakshmi, You grant to us all things that are auspicious.

ŌMKĀRA SVARŪPIṆI

Ōmkāra svarūpiṇi uṇarū
nīyente hṛdayāntarālaṅgalil
mṛdu tantriyil orumantramāy
ātmāvin varavīṇayil uṇarū
ōmkāra svarūpiṇi

O embodiment of OM, awaken. You who are the mantra that emanates from the soft strings of the veena of the Self in the depths of my heart, awaken.

Āhlādaniravinte malarvāṭiyil
sāmōdamāṭum mayūripōle
ānandanarttanam āṭān ninakente
jīvitārāma moruṅgi nīle

Like the garden filled with the happiness of a merrily dancing peacock, my life is ready for Your dance of bliss.

Pārippparakkunna pūttumbipōl kāti
lāṭikalikkunna pūvallipōl
kākalipāṭunna pūñchālapōl pāṭi
yāṭittimarkku kennātmāvil nī

Like a dragonfly which darts through the air, like the flower petal that flutters in the wind, like a small stream that rhythmically chants, You sing and dance in my Self.

ŌRŌ NIMIṢAVUM

Ōrō nimiṣavum eṇṇiyeṇṇi
nīṛunnitenuṭe janmam ammē
ālambahīnayī paitalingu
kēṇiṭunnammaye kāṇuvānāy

O Mother, I am burning as I count every moment of my life that passes away. This baby who has no other refuge is crying for his Mother.

Sachitānanda tarangiṇiye
māyā mahārṇṇava tāriṇiye
āśrita duḥkha nivāriṇiye
ammaye kāṇuvān kēṇīṭunnu

O Mother, You are the ocean of existence-consciousness-bliss. You take us across the ocean of transmigration. You remove the sorrows of those who take refuge in You. I am crying for the vision of You to dawn within my mind.

Etrayō sandhyakaḷ māññu pōyi
etrayō rātri dinaṅgaḷ pōyi
etrayō gāna sumaṅgal ammē
tṛppādam tēṭi piṭarnnu vīṇu

Countless twilights have faded away. Countless days and nights have come and gone. Countless songs have been offered at Your holy feet like flower blossoms.

Sachit sukhāmṛtavarṣiṇiyāy
sarva bhavāmaya hāriṇiyāy
sarva charāchara pālakiyāy
amma aṇayunnatētu nāḷil

O Mother, You shower the bliss of supreme consciousness upon us, You remove from us the precious illusions of vanity and pride and You are the protector of all. When will You come before me?

ŌṬI ŌṬI OLIVATENKE

Ōṭi ōṭi olivatenke tēṭi tēṭi nān kalaittēn
pāṭi pāṭi unai araittēn kaṇṇā kaṇṇā
nāṭi nīyum varuvatēntrō kaṇṇā kaṇṇā

Where have You run away to and hidden? I am exhausted from searching for You. I call out to You and sing Your name, Kanna, O my Kanna! When will You come before me, Kanna, O my Kanna!

Gōpiyarum inke nirka rādhaiyum en arukil nirka
kaṇṇan maṭṭum pōnatenkē kaṇṇā kaṇṇā
ennai kaṇkalanka vaippatum muraiyā kaṇṇā

All of the gopis are here and even Radha has come, but where have You gone, O Kanna, O my Kanna! Is it fair to leave us in sorrow, Kanna, O my Kanna!

Enku nī sentrālum ankellām unnai tēṭi
tanku taṭai illāmal kaṇṇā kaṇṇā - unnai
kaṇṭu kalittirukkum varam arulvāy kaṇṇā

O my Kanna! Grant me the boon that, wherever You go, I might follow and thus forever enjoy the sight of Your form before my eyes.

Uḷḷamenum peṭṭakattil urankiya rattinattai
ankuminkum tēṭi tēṭi kaḷaittēn kaṇṇā
ullattil māmaṇiyāy tikazhvāy kaṇṇā

I have become weary wandering here and there looking for the undiscovered gem in the treasure-chest of my heart, O Kanna. Be the crest-jewel of my heart, O my Kanna!

PĀLANA PARĀYAṆĪ AMṚTĒŚVARI

Pālana parāyaṇī amṛtēśvari
pāvana pūjitē jagadīśvari

Immortal Goddess, there is none other like You to protect us. Goddess of the universe, You are worshipped by pure souls.

Śrītajana manō rañjani
śrīmannagara nāyikē
pañcha tanmātra sāyakē
namāmi śrī lalitāmbikē

All who take refuge in You feel that their burdens are lifted. You reside in a most auspicious and prosperous city (the Sri Chakra.) You wield the five subtle elements (sight, touch, taste, smell and sound) as arrows. I bow to Sri Lalitambika.

Patita lōkō dhāriṇī
kali kanmaṣa nāśini
ābālagōpa vidhitē
namāmi śrī lalitāmbikē

You uplift those who have fallen and You remove the evils of this age. I bow to Sri Lalitambika who is well known to all.

PAṆDHARĪTSĀ DĒVĀ TUJHĀ

Paṇdharītsā dēvā tujhā
ārati ōvāḷude
śyāmā tujhī kṛpā sadā

āmhāvarī rāhudē

O Lord of Pandharpur, let us perform arati (worship) for You. O Shyama (one with a dark complexion), may Your blessings always be with us.

Hāth tūjhī kaṭēvarī
angāvarī pītambar
jīvamātsā charaṇī tujhyā
kṣaṇ bharī mātsā dēvā
ānandāt rāhudē
śyāmā tujhī krpā sadā
āmhāvarī rāhudē

You are standing with Your hands on Your waist and You wear glowing yellow attire. At least for a second, let my heart rest at the feet of Your divine form and thus feel happiness. May Your blessings be with us always.

Rakhumāyītsā dēvā vasō
rūp tujhā lōchanī
śōkpīḍhā charaṇī tujhē
kṛpā sadā mājhā dēvā
āmhāvarī vāhudē
śyāmā tujhī kṛpā sadā
āmhāvaṛī rāhudē

Let my eyes see Your form everywhere. All losses and pains can be faced when one is under Your protection and rests at Your feet. May Your blessings always be with us.

Sukh thōda dukh bhāri duniyā
hī bhalī buri
kaṣṭātsudhā tujhē manan
satat mī mātsā dēvā
ānandānī karūdē
śyāmā tujhī kṛpā sadā
āmhāvarī rāhudē

In this world of good and bad there are few joys but many sorrows. Let my mind bear all of the hardship in my life happily by remembering You. May Your blessings always be with us.

PĀṬIṬUVĀY MANAMĒ

Pāṭiṭuvāy manamē avan pukaḷ
nāṭiṭuvāy avan darśanamē

Sing His praise, O mind. Seek His darshan always.

Enkum nīyē etilum nīyē
eninum manatil nimmati enkē
tañcham un malarpādam en paṇintēnē
dayaipuri arulpuri anudinam nīyē

You are everywhere and in everything, yet I have no peace of mind. I strive to remember Your blessed feet. Have mercy on me and shower Your grace upon me every day.

Tiruvalar uruvāy chuṭarmigu oliyāy
paṇintiṭum ulamatil naṭamiṭa varuvāy
kanintiṭum mozhiyāy kavitayin poruḷāyi
ennil kalantiṭa ennai marantiṭa
karuṇai sey kaṇṇā

O beautiful and divine light, dance in this humble heart. You are sweet language and also poetry—merge me into that sweetness. Have mercy on me, O Kanna.

Ānandam paramānandam
kaṇṇanin tiruvuru darśanamē

The darshan of Kanna is the ultimate and supreme bliss.

PRĒM JŌ DIYŌ

Prēm jō diyō ta bār jēn
tanjī yād me magna makhē kajēn
muñchā prabha hē dayā ra pā
muñchā bhagavān jay śrīrām

O Lord, light the lamp of love in my heart, let me be immersed in the remembrance of You. O my Ram, embodiment of kindness, victory to You.

Bhaṭake tho man ghaṇā dakh dē thō
tōsā parē kithe khaṇī vanēthō
kṛpā kajēn muñchā rām (2x)
man mandira me rah jēn ta

As my mind is always wandering, it gives me nothing but sorrow. It takes me far away from You. Please have compassion on me, shower Your mercy in the temple of my heart.

Nagānō achēthō dhan bhina ṭhaye thī
rām hi rām bas chavaṇ achē thō
kṛpā kajēn muñchā rām (2x)
tuñchē darśan jī ās ā rām

I don't know any songs, nor do I know how to sing properly. I only know how to call out Your name. My dear Ram, bestow Your grace upon me.

Kṛpā kajēn muñchā rām (2x)
prēm jō diyō bār jēn aj

O my Lord Ram, bestow Your grace and light the lamp of love in my heart today.

PŪVURAṄGA TĀYĒ

Pūvuraṅga tāyē pozhuthuraṅga
puviyil ullorgalum āzhndhuraṅga
nī uraṅga innum maruppathum yeno
nithilamē nī kannuraṅgu

The world is asleep, the day has ended and everyone is fast asleep. Why do You still refuse to sleep? O Mother, please sleep.

Vanuraṅga mannuraṅga
vanavarpolum naṅguraṅga
vanjayudan ñan talattu pada
vadham seyyamal kannuraṅgu

Heaven and Earth are asleep and even the celestials are asleep. I am singing You a lullaby with all of my love so without argument please close Your eyes.

Pon muttu kattilitten pumalar thottilitten
anbudan vīsi arumbum vervai thudaitten
araro padivitten arul patham varudi vitten
kan valarvai kanne kan valarvai

I have arranged a golden cot decorated with flowers. I have fanned You with love, sang You a lullaby and caressed Your blessed feet. So, close Your eyes darling.

Kalaippiruthalum karuthamal adhanai
engulukkai nī uzhalvadhum yeno
poyyurakkam nī uraṅga un
malar pol vizhi adhanai
payyave nān mūda kannuraṅgu

Why are You toiling so hard for us without even considering how tired You are Yourself? You are only pretending to sleep so I am going to close Your eyes by myself. Please sleep well.

PYĀRĒ KĀNHĀ

Kānhā kānhā
tujhkō lōrī sunāvū sunāvū yaśōdā mayyā

My dear Kanna, let mother Yashoda sing You a lullaby and put You to sleep!

Pyārē kānhā mērē pyārē kānhā
bhōḷē kānhā mērē pyārē kānhā
nannī nannī ānkhōn mē nindiyā ṛāṇī
kab āyē kānhā tū sōjā kānhā

O darling, innocent Kanna, sleep has come to Your baby eyes. Go to sleep, Kanna!

Dinbhar tō khēlan kō dōdē kānhā
ab nanhē paiyā bōlē tū sōjā kānhā
dinbhar bansī kō sehlāyē kānhā
ab nanhē ānkha bōlē ta sōjā kānhā

All day long You ran and played but now Your baby feet are telling You to go to sleep. All day long You caressed Your flute and now Your baby hands are saying that You should fall asleep.

Dinbhar dilōn kō churāyē kānhā
ab nanhī ānkh bōlē tu sōjā kānhā
jagko has haskē behlāyē kānhā
ab nanhē honth bōlē ta sōjā kānhā

All day long You stole our hearts; now those innocent eyes say that You should sleep, Kanna! All day long You entertained the world with Your laughter but now those baby lips are saying to fall asleep.

Lōgōn kē prēm nit samāyē kānhā
tērā hṛdaya bhī ab bōlē tū sōjā kānhā

You filled the whole world with love and now Your own heart is telling You to sleep.

Kālī ghaṭā dhīrē sē chāyē kānhā
dēkhō vō bhī tō lōrī sunāyē kānhā
yamunā kī lahrē bhī gāyē kānhā
khal khal khal lahrōm kī lōrī kānhā

The dark clouds have slowly gathered in the sky, Kanna! Even they are singing lullabies to You. The waves of the Yamuna sing to the lapping, gentle lullaby of the river.

Bagiyan kē phū lōm kī mehk kānhā
tujhē bhāyē kānhā ta sōjā kānhā
pavanrāj jhula jhulāyē kānhā
tu sōjā kānā ab tō sōjā kānā

The flowers from the garden have brightened You, Kanna! The wind has come to rock You to sleep.

Yaśō mayyā kā lāl nandabābā kā bāl
gāyē lōrī rē yē jagsārā
lalā lalā lōrī kānhā tujhkō lōrī
sōjā sōjā kē tū hai jagpāl

Darling of Yashoda and Nanda, the whole world is singing a lullaby to You. O protector of the entire world, won't You please sleep?

RĀDHAI ULLA IṬATTIL

Rādhai ulla iṭattil ellām kaṇṇan allavā un
rāsagītam tannil avaḷum mayankavillayā
gītaisonna mozhiyil ellām nīyum illayā kaṇṇā
gītai kūṟum poruḷanaittum nīyē allavā

Is it not so that, wherever one finds Radha, there Krishna will also be present? O Kanna, is Radha not enthralled with Your song of love? Are You not in every word of the Gita, O Kanna. Are You not the essence that the Gita proclaims?

Gōpiyarkaḷ neñcham untan
mañchamallavā - kaṇṇā
gōpiyarum nīyum enṟrum onṟrē allavā
nallavayum allavayum nīyē allavā – kaṇṇā
nal manatil untan oḷi tankavillayā

Is it not so that You have made the hearts of the gopis Your home, O Kanna? Have not You and the gopis merged in one another forever? Are You not present in both the good and the bad, Kanna? Is it not Your light that shines in a good heart?

Aṭippatuvum aṇaippatuvum nīyē allavā – kaṇṇā
atan mūlam solluvatum vēdam allavā
manam unnai maṟaippatum māyai allavā kaṇṇā
manattirayai vilakkiviṭṭāl nīyē allavā – anku

You are the one who dispenses the results of actions. You are the essence about which the Vedas teach. Is it not Your maya that makes You disappear from our minds, O Kanna? When the veil of the mind is removed, You are seen to be everywhere.

RĀMAKṚṢṆA GŌVINDA

Rāmakṛṣṇa gōvinda nārāyaṇa hari
kēśavā murārī kēśavā murārī
pāṇduranga murārī pāṇduranga

Rama and Krishna, Lord Narayana, Keshava and Murari (names of Krishna), Lord Panduranga.

Lakṣmī nivāsa pāhē dīna bandhu
tujhā lāgo chandu sadā mājhē
murārī pāṇduranga

Abode of Lakshmi, refuge of the poor and the helpless, I beg for Your mercy. I pray that my mind sings the song of Your divine name.

Tukā maṇē mājhē hēnchigā mānkaṇē
akhaṇdha hī gāṇē nām tūjhē
murārī pāṇduranga

Tukaram says, "My only demand is that I should have the opportunity to sing Your name without interruption."

RĀM RĀM BŌLŌ JAY JAY

Rām rām bōlō jay jay
siyā rām bōlō

Victory to Ram! Chant the names of Sita and Ram.

Nām kō tērē nit gāyēngē
rimjhim rimjhim barsē nayanā
daras binā ab tō nahī jīnā

We'll chant Your name daily. Our tears are flowing profusely; we don't even want to live anymore without having Your darshan.

Dānavabaṇjana daśaratha nandana
dīnavatsalā rām
mahita mahēśvara chāpa dalankar
jānaki jīvana rām

You kill the evil demons, son of Dasaratha, and You protect the poor. You are famous for breaking the bow of Shiva. You are the life of Janaki (Sita).

Rām ō jay jay rām, ō jay jay rām
ō jay jay rām

Victory to Ram. Sing for victory to Sita and Ram.

Pitā kē vāk kō pālnēvālē kausalyātmaja rām
rāvaṇa darp kō tōḍnēvālē ayōdhyāvāsī rām
kālātmaka paramēśvara rāmā (jay jay jay rām)
bharadvāja mukha prārthita rām)
āyē ab tō dvārpē tērē
bhardē jhōlī har le andhērē

Kauslaya's son Ram, You fulfilled the oath taken by Your father. You dwell in Ayodhya. In Your confrontation with Ravana You destroyed his ego. You are beyond time and You are an incarnation of God. Bharadwaj Muni prayed only to You. Now we have come before Your door. Please bestow Your boons upon us and remove our darkness.

Dānavabaṇjana daśaratha nandana
dīnavatsalā rām
mahita mahēśvara chāpa dalankar
jānaki jīvana rām

You kill the evil demons, son of Dasaratha, and You protect the poor. You are famous for breaking the bow of Shiva. You are the life of Janaki (Sita).

Rām ō jay jay rām, ō jay jay rām
ō jay jay rām
(rām rām bōlō jay jay siyārām bōlō)

Victory to Ram. Sing for victory to Sita and Ram.

RŌTĒ JAG MĒ

Rōtē jag mē āyē thē
hastē jag sē jānā hē
kar kē yād sādā tujhē
parama pad kō pānā hē

We come into this earth crying but we should leave it with a smile on our face. Remembering You incessantly, Lord, we will become one with the supreme Truth.

Prēm kā ajñan lagā kē
dvēṣ bhāv miṭānā hē
dēkh tujhē sab kē dil mē
sabkā ādar karnā hē

Applying the balm of love, Lord, I want to remove all hatred within me. Seeing You residing in all hearts, enable me to treat all beings with respect.

Dukhōm kē ghērē mē bhī
mujhakō muskurānā hē

pās tērē ōr ānē kā
avasar inē banānā hē

Even in the midst of sorrows I wish to smile. I want to utilize my sorrows as opportunities to grow closer to You.

Sach nahī hē sāth kisī kā
man mē bōdh jagānā hē
samga rahōgē tum hī mērē
sumiran nit yē karnā hē

I want to kindle the awareness within that no support in this world is permanent. I wish to remember always that You alone will be eternally with me.

SĀGARA DĀLAKE

Sāgara dālake dina kara nilida
agalida hagalige vyathayēke
viśvaśilpiyā līlayidellā
viṣāda vētake nalinagalē

The sun has set in the western ocean and the day has started its lament. It is but the play of the universal architect. Why should the closing lotuses be dejected?

Akhilāṇḍarājana vinōdaramga
ī lōka śoka pūrṇṇa
sūtradagombe nānū alutihe
kambani miḍiyada śileyāgi

This world, full of misery and sorrow, is but a drama of the Lord. I remain as an onlooker. I am but a wooden puppet in His hands. I have no tears to shed.

Bēsara vēdane tālalāgade
hā entu rōdiside - enmana
nānā duḥkhada kaṭalina naṭuvē
tīrava kāṇade aledihenu

As if in a flame, my mind is burning in separation from You. I am tossed about in this ocean of grief unable to find the shore.

SANDHYA MAYAṄGUKAYĀY

Sandhya mayaṅgukayāy eṅgō
pakalin puñchiri māyukayāy
āzhiyil muṅgi āreyō tēṭān
ā jyōti bimbam marayukayāy

Evening is growing dim and the happiness of daytime is subsiding. The effulgent sun, having flown into the ocean as if to search for someone, disappears.

Tīrattil irulinte niral kaṇṭu
orēkāntapaphikan tēṅgukayāy
virahattil vēdana sahiyāte bhūmiyum
mukham pottininnitā kēzhukayāy

Having seen the shadow of darkness on the shore, one lonely traveler is sobbing. Unable to bear the separation from the sun, the earth covers its face and weeps.

Ī vanavīthiyil mānava kōṭikal
ēvarum ēkarennōrkunnatār
tīrāvyathakalāl tēṅgikarayunnu
dūrattatinnoli kēlppatuṇta

On this path through the forest of Maya there are innumerable beings. Who amongst them remembers that all are one? The anguish of unending sorrows can be heard like an echo from afar.

Lōkamē śōkamaya māṇennōtiya
pāvanāt mākalka nandi cholān
gad gadattāl vākuvyaktamallā mahā
mēdhāvlāsatte vāzhttuvānum

It was the great saints and sages who perceived this world as full of sorrow. To them should be given the gratitude of humanity. Speech, subdued by a feeling of awe, cannot describe the great power that animates this creation.

ŚARAVAṆA BHAVANE

Śaravaṇa bhavane vēl murukā
śiva śankara sutanē vēlazhakā
śaravaṇa bhava śiva śaktiyin maintā
kāttaruḷēṇam śrī skandā

O Sharavana Bhavane, O Muruka (Subramanya), Lord Shiva's darling, armed with a beautiful spear, Lord Skanda, protect us with Your grace.

Bāla murukan lōka rakṣakan
kāmākṣiyuṭe makanāy nī
enkaḷ tāy makanē aruḷvāy guhanē
śaravaṇa bhava śiva śaktiyin maintā
kāttaruḷēṇam śrī skandā

O child Muruka, You are the protector of the world, You are the son of Mother Kamakshi. Son of our Divine Mother, Lord Skanda, protect us with Your grace.

Ninte narttanam kāvaṭiyāṭṭam
en manassinte ānandam
vēlā yudhanē mayil vāhananē
śaravaṇa bhava śiva śaktiyin maintā
kāttaruḷēṇam śrī skandā

The kavati attam, Your graceful dance, brings such a great delight to my heart. Wielder of the spear, O Muruka, come riding on Your peacock. Son of our Divine Mother, Lord Skanda, protect us with Your grace.

Śivanu guruvām ṣaṇmuhkhanē nī
nityam stutikkum ōmkāram
sachidānandanē śivanandananē
śaravaṇa bhava śiva śaktiyin maintā
kāttaruḷēṇam śrī skandā

Shanmukha, You are the guru of Lord Shiva Himself. You are the Omkara, the eternal sound. You are truth, consciousness and bliss, darling of Shiva. Son of our Divine Mother, Lord Skanda, protect us with Your grace.

ŚATA KŌṬI VANDANAM

Śata kōṭi vandanam hṛdayādi vandanam
aruḷ jñāna poruḷē nī varadānam choriyū
tvarayārnnu tirayunnu karaḷtēṅgi karayunnu
kanivōṭen hṛdayattil uṇarvāy varū

Hundreds of millions of salutations to You! Heartfelt salutations to You who are the essence of eternal wisdom. Kindly shower Your gracious boons upon us. Eagerly I search everywhere for You, helplessly I bitterly weep. Kindly come to my heart.

Amṛtēśvari kāmya varadē varū varū

karaḷinte kiḷirnāvilamṛtam tarū
suragamgayāy svaramadhu māriyāy varū
varaḷunna mama jīvanudakam tarū

Immortal Goddess, fulfiller of our desires, come, come! Please pour Your nectar on the tender buds of this heart. As the heavenly Ganges, as the sweet melody of a rainfall, come, come! Please grace this dry life of mine with water.

Śaraṇāgatarkamma karuṇāmayi neñchil
uṛayunnoranubhūti rasamādhuri
oru gāna śalabham pōl mama mānasam sadā
tirayunnu tava snēhasumarājikaḷ

You are the compassionate one for those who have taken refuge in You. A sweet contentment fills this heart. Like the melody of a butterfly, my mind is always searching for the bouquet of the flowers of Your love.

Oru kāḷasarppam variññu kotti - karaḷu
kaṭayunna nombaramirul paratti
azhalamarn ātmāvil amṛtam taḷichamma
aruḷīṭū arulinte aruṇōdayam

As a poisonous snake coils and bites, the most bitter pain in this heart has spread darkness around me. Disperse this sorrow, shower nectar in my heart. Let wisdom dawn in me like the rising sun!

SNĒHA DŪTIYĀY

Snēha dūtiyāy tāṇiraṅgivan
āturākula bhūmiyil
āke lōkattin ammayāyi nī
āzhi chūzhumīyūzhiyil

You have come down to this sorrowful and disease-ridden earth as a messenger of love. You are the Mother of the entire universe, residing in this earth that is swallowed by the oceans.

Kāmya karmmaṅgal ācharī cheṅgaḷ
āzhnnu pōyāmayaṅgaḷil
pāpa hāriṇi nī hanikkaṇē
śōkajīvita ātana

By doing actions with a desire for the results we have been deeply immersed in sorrows. Remover of sins, please destroy the difficulties in this sorrowful life.

Jīvitōnnata bhāgadhēyamām
jñāna kaivalya dhāmamē
tēṅgum en manō dāhabhūmiyil
prēmam āriyāy peyyaṇē

You are the state of wisdom and liberation that is the highest purpose of life. In my yearning mind, a land of thirst, please shower love.

Prēmabhaktiyum mōhamuktiyum
ēki nī dayāvāridhē
bhāva śudhamen lōlahṛttaṭam
jñānadīptamākkīṭaṇē

O embodiment of mercy, granting the devotion of love and liberating me from delusion, enlighten my heart that is pure in intention.

ŚRĪ RĀGHAVAM

Śrī rāghavam daśarathātmajam apramēyam
sītāpatim raghukulānvaya ratnadīpam

ājānubāhum aravindadalāyatākṣam
rāmam niśācharavināśakaram - namāmi

O descendent of Raghu, son of Dasarata, You are established in a state beyond the senses. O husband of Sita, jeweled lamp of the Raghu dynasty, one with long arms and eyes like the petals of a lotus, O Rama, You destroy the darkness of those who wander in ignorance. I bow before You.

Raghupatē rāghavā rājā rāmā
Ō raja rāmā patita pāvana sītāpatē rāmā

O King Rama, head of the dynasty of Raghu, purifier of those who have fallen, You are the husband of Sita.

Daśaratha nandana rājā rāmā
kausalyātmaja sundara rāmā
rāmā rāmā jaya rājā rāmā
rāghava mōhana mēghaśyāmā

O King Rama, son of Dasaratha, beautiful Rama, child of Queen Kausalya, Victory to You, O Raghava, Your skin is the beautiful complexion of rain clouds.

Jay jay rām jay jay rām
patita pāvana sītāpatē rāmā

Victory to Rama, the purifier of those who have fallen and the husband of Sita.

ŚRĪ RĀMACHANDRA KṚPĀLU

Śrī rāmachandra kṛpālu bhajamana
haraṇa bhava bhaya dāruṇam
nava kañjalōchana kañjamukha kara
kañja pada kañjāruṇam

O blessed mind, always meditate upon Lord Sri Ramachandra who is full of compassion. He eliminates the fear of the cycle of birth and death. O mind, adore the beauty of His eyes that resemble the pink petals of a freshly bloomed lotus. Worship His lotus face and the delicate red lotus flowers of His hands and feet.

Kandarpa agaṇita amitachavi
navanīla nīrada sundaram
paṭapītamānahu tadhita ruchi śuchi
naumi janakasutāvaram

My sincere salutations to the handsome Lord Sri Ramachandra whose beauty excels innumerable cupids and whose bodily luster resembles dark, fresh rain clouds. My sincere salutations to the Lord who is clad in pure yellow silk garments and shines as brightly as lightning. Salutations to the Lord of Sita Devi, the divine daughter of king Janaka.

Bhaja dīnabanḍu dinēśadānava
daitya vamśa nikandanam
raghu nanda ānanda kanda kōśala
chandu daśaratha nandanam

O mind, meditate upon the glory of Lord Rama, the true friend of those who are in distress. He has destroyed the evil-minded demons by His prowess. My Lord is the son of king Dasaratha, He is the source of joy and pride to the house of Raghu and the shining descendant of the Kosala dynasty.

Śiramukuṭakuṇḍala tilakachāru
udāra amgavibhūṣaṇam
ājānubhuja śarachā padhara
samgrāma jitakhara bhūṣaṇam

O mind, meditate on Lord Rama who is adorned with the royal crown, charming earrings, an auspicious mark on His forehead and other elegant jewels on His blessed body. Always think of His tall majestic form holding the victorious bow and arrow with which he has destroyed the demonic enemies such as Khara and Dushana.

Iti vadatitulasīdāsa śankara
śēṣa muni mana rañjanam
mama hṛdaya kuñja nivāsakuru
kāmādi khala dala gañjanam

Tulsidas is thus glorifying his Lord Ramachandra who is supreme joy to Lord Shiva and to all the sages. Tulasidasa prays to his beloved Lord to constantly abide in the lotus heart of His devotee so that all the worldly desires and other blemishes can be destroyed completely.

SŪNĪ Ā DUNIYĀ

Sūnī ā duniyā sūnū ā jīvan
chōṭī gayā tame jēdī vṛndāvan
ēvī jalē virahānī agan
ujaṭi gayū mārū mananu madhuban

O Krishna, since You have left Vrindavan the entire city is deserted and so is my life. In the fire of separation the garden of my heart has been reduced to ashes.

Chōṭyō jagattē sāth mārō
jēdī thāmyō mē hāth tārō
na jōyu pāchū pharīnē kēmē
na dhāryū chūṭṭ śe sāth taro

The world simply abandoned me when I sought Your refuge, but I was not bothered by that. I had Your support that I thought was eternal. But now, You too have left me and gone away.

Bhūlī ne tanē bhūlī nā śakū
hayyā nē mārā kēmē samatsāvū
nām tārū hū lai na śakū
raṭī raṭī hū rahī jā ū

I try hard to forget You but I am not able to do so. How should I console my grieving heart? I am not even able to utter Your name; when I do so I am left drenched with tears.

SŪNI HE

Sūni he galiyā sūnā he jīvan
jab sē gayē tum tyaj vṛndāvan
aisē jalē birhā kī agan
ujad gayā mērā man kā madhuban

O Krishna, since You have left Vrindavan the entire city is deserted and so is my life. In the fire of separation the garden of my heart has been reduced to ashes.

Chōṭā jag nē sāth mērā jab
thāmā mē nē hath tērā
na dēkhā pīchē muṭkē kabhī
na ṭūṭē sōchā thā sāth tērā

The world abandoned me when I sought Your refuge but I was not bothered. I had Your support which I thought was eternal. But now, You too have left me and gone away.

Bhūl kē bhī tuchē bhūl na pāvū
dil kō mē kaisē samjhāvū

nām tērā bhī lē na pāvū
rōtē rōtē me rah jāvū

I try hard to forget You but I am not able to do so. How should I console my grieving heart? I am not even able to utter Your name; when I do so I am left drenched with tears.

SUN MĒRĪ

Sun mērī maiyā māt bhavāni
jag jananī mahārāṇi
vinati sunō kalyāṇī

O Mother of the universe, kindly hear my prayer.

Bīt gayē ēsē janma yē kitnē
rahā tērī khōj mē sadā
ōr na rakhnā dūr mā mujhkō
ab tō galē sē lagālō mā
mamtā mē nahalāvō

How many lifetimes have passed away in the same manner as my present life is passing, Mother? I search for You always. Please do not keep me away from You any longer. Hold me close to You and bathe me in Your love.

Kehlānē kō tērī santān
guṇ mā kōyi mujhmē nahī
bēṭā chāhē hō jēsā bhī
mā mē he karuṇā hī
kartī he vō kṣmā hī

Even though I am Your child, Mother, none of Your virtues exist in me. Yet it does not matter what are the defects of the child; Mother is the embodiment of compassion and She forgives us and grants us Her grace.

Ājāvō mātē darśan dō

Please come, Mother, and grant us the vision of You.

ŚVĒTA PATMĀSANĒ ŚĀŚVATĒ

Śvēta patmāsanē śāśvatē ślāganīyē
śvēta patmāsanē

O Devi, seated in a white lotus flower, You are immortal and are worthy of our praise.

Sajjana hṛdsthitē vandanīyē
nirjjara sēvitē vijña nīyē
jananī dukhada bhava vāridi
kayarān vazhiyaruluka dēvi

O Devi, You reside in the hearts of the virtuous. Fountain-head of wisdom, You are served by the celestial beings. O Mother, kindly show the way to transcend the endless suffering of repeated birth and death.

Chittamām vairiye mattanākum
sattē marakkunna taskkaranmar
mada matsara krōdhāgraha
rāgādikala kaluka vēṇam

O Mother, desire, anger, pride and jeolousy are thieves who hide Your real essence. Dispel them from my heart.

Praṇavākṣarī jagal prāṇa mūrttē
praṇamicchiṭunnū dāsō ham
aruṇābhayil amarum oli –
tiralum tava darśanam aṇayān

O Devi, You are the essence of the sacred syllable "OM." You are the life in the universe. This servant prostrates before You to gain a vision of Your splendid, brilliant, red-hued form.

ŚYĀM VARṆĀ

Rādhē śyām rādhē śyām
rādhē śyām rādhē śyām
rādhē śyām rādhē śyām bōl
rādhē śyām rādhē śyām bōl

Sing to Radhe and Shyam.

Śyām varṇā sundarāngā
rādhikā samēdhā
vāsudēvā vēṇu lōlā
rāsa kēli lōla

Endowed with a body of a beautiful blue color, O companion of Radha, son of Vasudeva, sweetly You play the flute and dance the Rasa dance.

Yāda vēndrā nandalālā
kāma kōṭi ramyā
mañju hāsā māna sēśā
mādhavā murārē

Lord of the Yadavas, son of Nanda, beautiful one, blessed with an enchanting smile, You are the Lord of our hearts. You are Vishnu, the husband of Laksmi. You destroyed the demon Mura.

Padma nābhā pītachēlā
pāhimām ramēśā
gōkulēśā gōpabālā
gōpa vṛndanāthā

The lotus springs from Your navel and yellow robes adorn Your form. Please protect me, O Lord of Laksmi. Lord of Gokula, cow-herd boy, You are the Lord of the cow herders.

Viśva rūpā vēda vēdyā
tvat padābjam vandē
dēva dēvā dīna nāthā
dēhimangalam mē

Your form encompasses the universe. Your knowledge is as expansive as the Vedas. Salutations to Your lotus feet. O Lord of the meek, grant me auspiciousness.

TAN MAN DHAN NŪ

Tan man dhan nū karā mē arppaṇ
mā dē charaṇa vich arppit ē jīvan

I surrender my body, mind and wealth. My life I offer at Your holy feet, O Mother.

Tvāḍī bhakti dā mērē kōle dhan
tvāḍī sēvā dē layī mā ē tan
tvāḍē nā vich ḍubē chañchal ē man
mā dē charaṇā vich arppit ē jīvan

The only wealth that I possess is my devotion to You. The only use this body of mine has is to engage in Your service. Let this troubled mind drown in the sweet nectar of Your name. My life I offer at Your holy feet, O Mother.

Charon diṣa to ghere hege duṣman
ahankar māya vich fāṣya man
omkar da mā dē dē hun darṣan
mā dē charaṇā vich arppit ē jīvaṇ

From all directions I am surrounded by enemies. Pride and delusion have overpowered my mind. O Mother, please give me the vision of the Supreme. I offer my life at Your holy feet, O Mother.

Hun sirf hegī tvāḍī karuṇā dī lagan
jadō tvāḍē nā dā karā mē manan
tadō ṭhaṇḍī hōgī dil dī ē agn
mā dē charaṇā vich arppit ē jīvan

My only desire is for Your compassion. Only when I chant Your holy name will peace fill my heart. My life I offer at Your holy feet, O Mother.

TARŪ NĀM

Hē rām hē rām
andhārā jagmā dē ujās
āk tārū nām rē mārē man
sāchū dhan tārū nām rē

O Ram, please shine Your light into this dark world. Your name is truly a treasure. It is always present in my mind.

Tarū nām tārū nām tāru nām rē
mārē man sāchu dhan tārū nām rē
mārē man ēkādhār mārē man ēkādhār
tāru nām tāru nām tāru nām rē

In my mind the true treasure is Your name, only Your name. The only support for my mind is Your name.

Bigḍē banāvē kām tārū nām rē
bhavpār karē nāv tārū nām rē
mārē man vālu nām tārū nām rē
mārē man sāchū dhan tārū nām

Your name will help us to emerge from misfortune. It will carry the boat of this life across the ocean of the world to the other shore of eternity. Your name is dear to me; it is the true treasure of my mind.

Duḥkha dūr karē nām tāru nām rē
duḥkhi yō no ādhār ēk tārū nām rē
nām tārū prāṇpyārū tārū nām rē
nām tārū prāṇpyārū tārū nām

Your name takes away the sorrows from my mind. It is the only solace for the suffering masses of humanity. I hold Your name as the sweetest thing that I know of.

TAVA TIRUMOZHIKAḶ

Tava tirumozhikaḷ hṛdi tirumadhuram
śruti vachanāmṛta laharimayam
pularoḷi tiraḷum kuvalaya nayanam
hṛdi timirāpaha mihirakaram

Your sacred words are very sweet to my heart. The tune and words of the song are fascinating. Your beautiful eyes are like the morning sunrise. Please remove the darkness of my heart.

Kaivalyadāyini nin kṛpānugraham
kaiśōra kāntiyil nīntippū mānasam
avyāja divyamā pīyūṣapānattāl
mṛtyuvum mitramāyi tīrumallō dṛḍham

Kind one, from whom flow many blessings, grant me liberation. My mind is swimming in the ocean of light that is Your true being. Even death will become our friend if we can drink in Your unconditional love.

Aṇu jīvanāyi hṛttil maruvunnu nī
viśvamoru pādadhūḷiyāl virachippū nī
tānu mānasangaḷkku tuṇayāya chaitanya
mahimāvu nī jñāna savitāvu nī

You live in the center of my being. Just the sand from Your feet is enough for You to utilize in creating a universe. You are the power that animates our body and mind. You grant good things and knowledge.

Mozhiyilum mizhiyilum vazhiyunnu hā
viśva vijayiyāyi divyamā snēhadhāra
oru tirināḷamā ammē tavāntika
teriyaṭṭe jīvanā snēhavāypil

Your words and eyes are like flowers in which flows the divine love that can conquer the world. May I always stay near You, a small light that receives Your life giving love.

TĒRI KṚPĀ SĒ

Tērī kṛpā sē bēḍā pār hō
mērī mā tērī jay jaykār hō
dīn duḥkhī pāpī ōr rōgī
sab kā hī uddhār hō
mērī mā tērī jay jay kār hō

By Your Grace, may this raft reach the safety of the shore. May all those who are suffering and grieving, all those who have lived in a misguided manner, be uplifted. Victory to You, my Mother.

Sās sās mē tujhkō pujū
āṭh yām lū tērā nām
jab jīvan kī sanḍyā āyē
kṛpā karō mujh par avirām (2x)

With my every breath I worship You. Throughout the entire day I chant Your name. When the twilight of my life arrives please continually shower Your Grace upon me.

Hō bhaktīmay pal pal mērā
hō bhaktīmay jīvan śyām
jāvu kahā taj charaṇa tumhārē
pāvu inhī mē chārō dhām (2x)

Please grant that in each moment of my life I will feel devotion to You. If I were to wander from Your holy feet, where would I go? May I fulfill all of the duties of my life without forgetting Your blessed feet.

Jay jaykār jay jaykār
maiyā tērī jay jaykār
sunlē mērē dil kī pukār
jay jaykār jay jaykār
maiyā tērī jay jaykār

Victory to You, Mother, the whole world is singing Your praises. Please listen to the call of my heart.

TĒRĒ SIVA

Tērē siva kōn hai sāth ab na chōdō
kanhā mērā hath ab na chōdō

Who is there other than You, Krishna? Don't let go of me now, don't let go of my hand.

Virahā kī āg nē kyā kabhī tujhē jalāyā
rotē rotē kisī kī yād me rāt kabhī bitāya
dil ka dard bujhānē vālē
dard na pēhchānē
kis liyē hum jiyē – hāyē
maut kyōm na āyē

Have You ever been burnt in the fire of separation? Have You spent long nights crying for someone? You are the only one who can ease this heartache, yet You seem not to have noticed it. Then what is it that I still live for, Krishna? Why doesn't death come for me?

Khēl tēra bas hai kanhā
khīl sē thak gayē ham
apnē banākē mujhko
bhūl ab gayē kyōm
dardē dil hai tū kyā jānē
ōr kisē sunāūmōr kisē pukarū

Enough of Your play, I am weary of it now. Having made me Yours, why have You now forgotten me? To whom can I call out? Who will understand the pangs of this aching heart? Whom else can I call?

TĪN GUṆO

Tīn guṇo kī tērī kāyā
tīn guṇō kī māyā
jag jīvan tū jīs kō samajhē
tērē man kī chāyā
rē bandē (4)

Your body is composed of the three qualities of nature. Even this illusory world is of the same qualities. What you perceive as the Earth and your life on it is all but a reflection of your mind.

Khōj rahā bāhar tū jis kō
vāsī antar man kā
rūp samāyā sab mē us kā
tū nē hī bil gāyā
rē bandē (4)

That which you search for outside of yourself is, in reality, the essence that is within you. It is present in all forms. You have created what appears as a separation between you and your soul.

Tērī tṛṣṇā nē bun ḍālē
jāl tirē bhar mō kē
bhāv sabhī sukh dukh prāṇī
upaj tire karamō kē
kāraṇ tū ap nī mastī kā
khud kō tū nē rūlāyā
tīn guṇō kī tērī kāyā
tīn guṇō kī māyā
rē bandē (4)

Your desires have woven the net of your delusions. All of your imaginings, your sorrows and joys, are all products of your own actions. You are the cause for your own happiness or tears of sorrow. Your body is composed of the three qualities of nature. Even this illusory world is of the same qualities.

Ghaṭ ghaṭ prāṇī prāṇī mēn
pahachān tū ap nā svāmī
kis kō ap nē rāg sunā yē
vō tō antaryāmī
ghaṭ apnī antar mastī kā
tūnē kyō chalkāyā
tīn guṇō kī tērī kāyā
tīn guṇō kī māyā
rē bandē (4)

In all beings, in all vessels, recognize your Lord. To whomever you tell your tales of woe, the Lord is the indweller. Why have you lost your way to your inner spirit comprised of joy? Your body is composed of the three qualities of nature. Even this illusory world is of the same qualities.

TIRUVADI TĒṬI

Tiruvadi tēṭi vanden vel muruga
kāvaṭi vanden māl maruka
kannir kural kēṭṭu vā muruga
kann kaniya darisanam tā muruga

O Muruga, I have come in search of Your divine feet. Nephew of Lord Vishnu, hear my cry and come before me. Grant the vision of Your form to my yearning eyes.

Ṣanmukhan unṭan śaraṇam tēṭi vel muruga
sakalamum marandu padaivida-
dainden māl muruga
aṇṭa charācharam anudinam
tutikkyum vel muruga
adiye kural keṭṭudanē viraivāy māl muruga

Shanmukha, I have forsaken rest in my search for You. You are the Lord who is worshipped every day by all the beings in the universe. Hearing my prayers, please come before me.

Mōhana rūpā kumarā azhagā
manasumai nīkkida vā vā muruga

Your spellbinding form is ever young and handsome. Come before me, Muruga, and free me from my burden of sorrows.

Panniru vizhiya pazhani
puri vāzha vel muruga
pār kadal vāsan sodari tanayā māl muruga
marutalam mīt mazhai nīr pōle vel muruga
pazhamudir cholayin ālayam
pukharum māl muruga

O Lord with twelve eyes, who lives in the Palavi hills, relative of the Lord of the ocean, You are fresh like a shower of rain. You reside in the Palamuthir Cholai shrine.

TRILŌKA MĀTṚ RŪPINI

Trilōka mātṛ rūpini
trilōchanē trivargadē
mahēśī maṅgalātmikē
manōjña nṛtya lōlupē

Your form is that of the Mother of the three worlds, with three eyes (the spiritual eye is the third eye), and You grant the three boons (material attainments, moral or dharmic attainments and spiritual attainments or realization.) Great

Goddess, essence of auspiciousness, You enjoy enchanting and beautiful dancing.

Anahatabja samsthitē
viśudhi chakra vāsini
śivankari sudhāmayi
samastha saukya dāyini

Seated in the anahata lotus, residing in the vissudhi chakra, accomplishing auspicious deeds, O embodiment of nectar, You bestow all happiness.

Bhavāni bhakta vatsalē
puratrayēṣvari umē
chaturbhujē bhajāmyaham
bhavat padāmbhujē dvayam

Mother Bhavani, full of motherly love for Your devotees, Goddess of the three worlds, O Uma, adorned with four hands, I worship Your two holy feet.

Girīndra nandinī śivē
bhayāpahē jayapradē
bhavabdhi tārini jayē
smarāmi tē padambujam

Daughter of the Himalayas, auspicious one, remover of all fear, You grant us victory. You guide us across this vast and dangerous ocean of our worldly life. I strive to remember Your blessed feet.

Jay jagadambē jay jagadambē jay jagadambē mā

Victory to the Mother of the Universe, victory to the Mother of the Universe.

ULLAM ENUM

Ullam enum dīpattilē
unmai enum neyyūtri
anai untan kōvililē
azhakāka ētri vaittēn

In the lamp of my heart I pour the oil of truth. I then light it before You, O Mother.

Ētri vaitta dīpattilē
en ammā nī varuvāy
iṭar āzhi nīnkiṭavē
chuṭar āka nīyiruppāy

In that burning light, O Mother, You are the effulgence that removes all of the darkness in my mind and all of the difficulties in the path of my life.

Vān tīyāy mārutamāy
maṇ nīrāy nirppavalē
vāzhum makkal tuyar tīrkka
vān mazhaiyāy vandiṭuvāy

It is You, O Mother, who pervades the elements of this universe. You shower Your Grace and thus remove the sorrows of the people.

Ēzhaikku manam iranki
emai kākka vārāyō
enkum nirai umaiyavalē
enai kaṭaikkaṇ pārāyō

O Mother, won't Your heart melt looking at the pitiful sight of this son of Yours? O all-pervasive One, won't You bestow Your grace on me with a merciful glance?

UL URAIKINṬRA

Ul uraikinṭra porul enṭrum azhikiṭratillai
avan anṭri oru aṇuvum asaikinṭratillai
ullukul atusirittāl nammil varum māttam
jīvātman tānnazhutāl gatiyil varum ētram

The indwelling principle never perishes. Without Him (the Lord) not even an atom can move. When That which dwells within smiles upon us there will be an inner change. When the individual soul cries for emancipation there will be salvation.

Aṭaiyāta peruvāzhva vāzhantum payanillai
tun bankal illāmal peruvāzhavum ilai
tuṇai śērum porul yāvum nilaiyānatilai
nilaiyilai enṭrālum utavāmalilai

Even if one leads a great and successful life there is still no escape from suffering. None of the objects around us are permanent. Their use is only temporal.

Ulkankal yāvum kanavenṭra solvar
kanavenṭra sonnālum kāṇāmal ilai
irukinṭra pōt nammai parikinṭra māyam
tanaiviṭṭa silar tannai tēṭāmalilai

It is said that all the worlds are but a dream. That may be so; yet still we experience them as real. Maya catches hold of us without fail. Only a few remain who search for the eternal Truth.

Kāmattin koṭuvāzhva tira vāmalilai
tirantālum aṭayka vazhī illāmalilai
kuttankal palaseyta tiruntiviṭṭā oruvan
īśvaranin padamatanai aṭayāmalilai

Desire inflicts everyone with its passion. In spite of that there is a hope for escape. Even a person who has committed many sins can repent and thus attain the feet of the Lord

Anainattilum vilankum param porulē nī ezhuka
iruntum illātirukum uravē nī varuka
vēṇṭāta vinaiyanaittum ennai viṭṭa vilaka
avan kamalamalar tāl paṇiya guruvarulai taruka
sadguru varulai taruka

O supreme principle , dwelling within all beings, appearing as non-existent even though You exist, awake! To transcend my sins and my fate, to attain to His lotus feet, may I attain the grace of the Satguru. May that grace be showered upon me.

UN KAIYIL PILLAI

Un kaiyil pillai ena nān māṛavā
ennil un anpai nī parimāravā
oru muttam tirumuttam tara nīyum vā ammā
atai nittam nān peravum varam īyavā

O Mother, may I become a baby in Your arms. Come and fill me with Your love. Give me a divine kiss. May I receive that blessing forever with Your grace.

Un kōvil paṭiyāka nān māravā
unnaṭiyār tiruvadikal talai chūṭavā
un pādatūliyāka nān māravā ammā
nal vēda porulai ni unarthīda varai
nān amṛtēśvari tṛppādam talai chūtavā

May I be the doorstep to Your temple, Mother, and may my head be blessed with the touch of the feet of Your devotees. Let me be the dust on Your feet. Let the essence of the four Vedas live on through me. May I bear the holy feet of the immortal Goddess on my head.

Tirumārbil tikazhmālai nān ākavā
tirumēni sugandhatte nān kūravā
abhiṣēka porul āka nān māravā
un anpāna inimayil nān dinam mūzhkavā
nān amṛtēśvari tṛppādam talai chūtavā

May I be a shining garment on Your divine form that exudes a sweet fragrance. Let me be the articles used in the bath and worship of Your feet. May I soak daily in the sweetness of Your love. May I bear the holy feet of the immortal Goddess on my head.

Un kayil thavazhum ṣir seyakava
arul kūri vinai tīrkum nal amuthakuvai
un sannidhi karppūram nān ākavā - ammā
oḷichinti nān karaintu unatākavā
nān amṛtēśvari tṛppādam tallai chūtavā

Let me be the prasadam in Your divine hand. Allow me to experience Your grace that helps us to overcome the miseries of life. May I be the camphor that is burnt in Your presence and may I thus dissolve into You. May I bear the holy feet of the immortal Goddess on my head.

UNNAI TĒṬI ULAKELLĀM

Unnai tēṭi ulakellām tuti pāṭuṭē – inpam
tanai tantu emaikākum amṛtēśvari

O Mother, the whole world searches for You and sings Your praises. Immortal Goddess, You are the one who grants bliss to me and protects me.

Unaiyenni ētu seya munaikinṭra pōtum
vinai mutru perum entra ninai vuṇṭu neñchil
maraiyāvum pōṭrum nal muzhumutar porule unai
maravāta nilaiyenṭrum taruvāy amutē

Whatever action I attempt while remembering You will surely produce a good result. So long as I have memory, I should never forget the supreme Self that is praised by all the scriptures. This state You should kindly grant, O divine nectar!

Karaiyinṭri nadiyillai maṇam inṭri malarillai
nīriṇṭri mukhilillai niyinṭri nān illai
nilaiyāmai nityam enpatai neñcham kāṇā
nilaiyinṭri inkunṭu nilaikol en neñchil

Just as there can be no river without a shore, no flower without fragrance, and no cloud without water, in the same way there is no me without You. Let my mind behold the impermanent nature of this world and let it be established in that which is eternal.

VANDANA KARŪ MĒ

Vandana karū mē tēri
mukh mē he tērā nām
jag kē tum pālan kartā
tum hō kṛpā nidhān

O Lord Ganesha, I prostrate to You and continuously chant Your holy name. O compassionate one, You control the whole of creation.

Jay gaṇēśa jay gaṇēśa jay gaṇēśa dēvā
sachē mīt tum hī mēre he gaurī nandana

Hail to You, great Lord Ganesha. You alone are my only true refuge.

Nām mē tēre hē śakti
sumiran sē milē bhakti
ēk hi tujhsē he vinati
tujh mē līn rahē mati

Your divine name has so much power. The repetition of it bestows one with devotion. O Lord, I request You to never let my mind wander but let it be filled with thoughts of You.

Vyāpt jagat mē rahtē hō
vyakt bhī tō hō jāvō
man mandir mē darśan dēkar
andhakār bujhā jāvō

Though You are omniscient my Lord, I have the earnest desire to see You. So please appear before me in Your adorable form. Be enshrined in my heart forever; that alone will destroy all of the darkness within me.

VARADĒ VARADĒ AMṚITĀNANDAMAYI MĀ VARADĒ

Varadē varadē amṛitānandamayi mā varadē

O Mother of immortal bliss, bestow boons upon us!

Vīṇā vādini vidyādāyini
vēdavidhāyini varadē
Sakala kalāmayi sāma vinōdini
gānavilōle varadē
Tuṣāradhavalē sāttvikacharitē
śvētāmbari mā varadē
Pustaka hatē patmajadayitē
bhaktavatsalē varadē

Playing upon the veena, imparting the boon of knowledge, creator of the Vedas, shower boons upon us. Abode of all of the arts, You enjoy the music of the Sama Veda and You revel in singing. Bestow boons upon us. Your complexion is as white as snow, and You are clothed in pure white garments. O Mother of a taintless nature, bless us with boons. You hold a book in Your hand, O companion of Lord Brahma. It is well known that You are affectionate to Your devotees. Thus shower boons upon us.

VAZHI DŪRAM

Vazhi dūram kurayunnīliṭayil ñāne viṭetti
aṟiyunnīliṭaneññil iruḷ tiṅgunnu
aṟiyāte mizhiyōram nanayunnu – tirujñāna –
poruḷē pūnkaraḷil ponnoḷi tūkumō

Having almost reached the end of my path I struggle not to lose my way. Darkness floods my heart and my eyes fill with tears. Omniscient one, please fill my soul with golden light.

Mazhamēgham kaniyāte
ozhiyumbōl kurul kāññu
karayāte karayunni – torum chātakam

tiruvuḷḷam kaniññente karaḷinte varaḷnāvil
choriyillē - uṇarvinte teḷinīrkkaṇam

The chataka bird is in deep sorrow when the rain clouds pass by without dispensing any rain. Will You show mercy to me and shower the pure water of wisdom on my dried heart?

kuḷirōḷam tazhukunna puzhayōram pōlente
karaḷ tīram tazhukān nin karatāreṅgō
izha pōyoruṭupam pōl ulayunnen hṛdayam nin
karameṅg - karayeṅg jagadambikē

Like the river banks are caressed by the cool currents, where is Your hand to caress my heart? Like a cloth that has lost its thread, my heart has been undone. O Mother of the universe, where is Your hand and where is the bank?

VIRAHA KĪ BĀDAL

Viraha kī bādal he chāyi
rulāti he mujhe tanhāyi
pūch tī hū śyām piyārē
yē kēsi lambī judāyī

Gray clouds of separation are spread in the sky and loneliness makes me weep. I ask You, my dearest Shyam, how long can You allow this separation?

Baiṭhī hū jamunātaṭ par
jānkar bhī tum nahī hō
kyā karū mānē na dil
kahtā he tum yahī hō

I sit on the banks of the Yamuna river and I wait. I know that You are far away and yet my heart will not listen to me; it tells me that You are right here with me.

Yād bhi chute nahī
ās bhī tute nahī
kyo he vo hamse rute
jane bhī koi nahī

The fond memories of the Lord do not leave me. Neither does my yearning decline. Why is He angry at me? Nobody knows the reason.

Kaliyā bhī khiltī nahī
kōyal bhi gatī nahī
śyām binā vṛndāvan kē
jīvan mē sangīt nahī

The flowers have stopped blossoming; the nightingale has stopped singing. Without You, my Shyam, there is no music in Vrindavan.

Murali bajate āna
payal jhankate āna
jag utega vṛndāvan
ayega phirse jīvan
or na tum tarasana
śyāmji śyāmji śyāmji tum chale āna

Come before us, O my Lord, playing Your flute. Let me hear the sound of Your anklets. Hearing these sounds, all of Vrindavan will come to life and awaken. Do not delay any further. O Krishna, please come back soon.

VIRAHANOMBARA

Virahanombara kathayura cheyum
karalin gadgadambāṣpam
janani nin padatāriṇa tazhuki
ozhukum vanakulyakaḷāy

Mother, my heart sheds tears in its pain of separation from You. These tears have become a stream that washes Your blessed feet.

Hṛdayahāriyām kavitapōl sāndram
ozhukum naṛutēn mozhikal
karalukuṭayum kātara jīvita
nōvinatauṣadhalahari janani
nīyāṇennuṭe dhyēya manōhara
mōhana vigrahamennum pūjita
śōbhana vigrahamennum

Mother, Your honey-sweet words flow like poetry that captures my heart. Your words are the medicine for the wrenching pain of our lives. My mind always centers on You, You are the beautiful, captivating, shining idol for me to meditate on and worship.

Divya sumōpama sundaravadanam
vara prasādam tūki
viriyumō tava viraha vyathayil
hṛdayameriyāte – janani
nīyenmānasavīnayil mōhana
gānāmṛtam āyuṇarū – nirmala
snēhāmṛtam āyuṇarū

Mother, will Your divine face, beautiful as a flower, blossom in my heart? Will it shower its blessings and thus dispel all pain? Mother, awake as a beautiful song in the veena of my heart, awake as the nectar of love.

Chants

AṆṆAPŪRṆA STŌTRAM

Nityānandakarī varābhayakarī
saundaryaratnākarī
nirdhūtākhila ghōra pāvanakarī
pratyakṣa māhēśvarī
prālēyāchala vamśa pāvanakarī
kāśīpurādhīśvarī
bhikṣām dēhi kṛpāvalambanakarī
mātānnapūrṇēśvarī//1//

O Mother Annapoorneshvari, please bestow alms upon me. You dispense eternal happiness as well as boons and protection. Our fears are dispelled by You. By washing away our sins You grant us mental purity. O great goddess, You purified the race of Himavan. Ruler of Kasipura, You are the embodiment of mercy.

Nānāratna vichitrabhūṣaṇakarī
hēmāmbarāḍambarī
mūktāhāra vilambamāna
vilasadvakṣōjakumbhāntarī
kāṣmīrā guruvāsitā ruchikarī
kāśīpurādhīśvarī
bhikṣām dēhi kṛpāvalambanakarī
mātānnapūrṇēśvarī//2//

O Mother Annapoorneshvari, please bestow alms upon me. Your hands are adorned with ornaments and jewels and You are beautifully clothed in golden attire. Upon Your breasts and waist rest garlands made of pearl. You are wonderfully fragrant with the frankincense of Kashmir, O incarnation of beauty. Ruler of Kasipura, You are the embodiment of mercy.

Yōgānandakarī ripukṣayakarī
dharmārthaniṣṭhākarī
chandrārkānalabhāsamānalaharī
trailōkyarakṣākarī
sarvaiśvarya samastavāñchitakarī
kāśīpurādhīśvarī
bhikṣām dēhi kṛpāvalambanakarī
mātānnapūrṇēśvarī//3//

O Mother Annapoorneshvari, please bestow alms upon me. You dispense the bliss of Yoga. By Your grace our enemies are destroyed and our feet are set firmly on the path of dharma. You display the radiance of the moon, the sun and fire. The three worlds are protected by You. All prosperity and all of the rewards for penance flow from You. Ruler of Kasipura, You are the embodiment of mercy.

Kailāsāchala kandarālayakarī
gaurī umā śaṅkarī
kaumārī nigamārthagōcharakarī
ōmkārabījākṣarī
mōkṣadvārakapāṭapāṭanakarī
kāśīpurādhīśvarī
bhikṣām dēhi kṛpāvalambanakarī
mātānnapūrṇēśvarī//4//

O Mother Annapoorneshvari, please bestow alms upon me. You dwell amidst the caves of Mount Kailash. O Uma, You radiate a golden hue. Consort of Lord Shiva, blessed with eternal youth, You reveal the inner meaning of the Vedas. Embodiment of 'OM,' You open the door to eternal liberation. Ruler of Kasipura, You are the embodiment of mercy.

Dṛśyādṛśya prabhūtapāvanakarī
rahmāṇḍabhāṇḍodarī
līlānāṭaka sūtra bhēdanakarī
vijñānadīpāṅkurī
śrī viśvēśāmanaḥ prasādanakarī
kāśipurādhīśvarī
bhikṣām dēhi kṛpāvalambanakarī
mātānnapūrṇēśvarī//5//

O Mother Annapoorneshvari, please bestow alms upon me. You grant all visible and invisible blessings. The entire universe is contained in You. This world is a drama that You have staged. You are the fire in the torch of wisdom. The mind of the Lord of the universe is pleased by You. Ruler of Kasipura, You are the embodiment of mercy.

Urvīsarvajanēśvarī bhagavatī
mātānnapūrnēśvarī
veṇīnīlasamānakuntalahari
nityānnadānēśvarī
sarvānandakarī daśā śubhakarī
kāśīpurādhīśvarī
bhikṣām dēhi kṛpāvalambanakarī
mātānnapūrṇēśvarī//6//

O Mother Annapoorneshvari, please bestow alms upon me. You are the queen of the world. Showering Your motherly love on all, You insure success. O ocean of kindness, with locks of beautiful hair arranged in braids, You provide the means of sustenance to all beings. Granting salvation to all, Your every action is auspicious. Ruler of Kasipura, You are the embodiment of mercy.

Ādikṣānta samasta varṇanakari
śambhōstri bhāvākarī
kāśmīrā trijanēśvarī trilaharī
nityāṅkurā śarvarī
kāmākāṅkṣakarī janōdayakarī
kāśīpurādhīśvarī
bhikṣām dēhi kṛpāvalambanakarī
mātānnapūrṇēśvarī//7//

O Mother Annapoorneshvari, please bestow alms upon me. The letters of the alphabet were first invented by You. You monitor Shambu's three-fold aspect of creation, protection and destruction. Covered in saffron, partner of the three-eyed destroyer of Tripura, ruler of the universe, You perfect in Yourself the beauty of the night and You open wide the doors to heaven. Ruler of Kasipura, You are the embodiment of mercy.

Dēvī svarṇa vichitraratnakhachitā
dakṣē karē samsthitā
vāmē svādupayōdharī sahacharī
saubhāgya māhēśvarī
bhaktābhīṣṭakarī dṛṣā śubhakarī
kāśīpurādhīśvarī

bhikṣām dēhi kṛpāvalambanakarī
mātānnapūrṇēśvarī//8//

O Mother Annapoorneshvari, please bestow alms upon me. O radiant one, adorned with a display of rare jewels, charming daughter of Daksha, You are blessed with perfect manners and noble virtues. Always engaged in auspicious acts, You grant the desires of those who earnestly open their hearts to You. Ruler of Kasipura, You are the embodiment of mercy.

Chandrārkānala kōṭikōṭisadṛśā
chandrām śubimbādharī
chandrārkāgni samāna kuṇḍaladharī
chandrārkavarṇēśvarī
mālāpustakapāśakāṅkuśadharī
kāśipurādhīśvarī
bhikṣām dēhi kṛpāvalambanakarī
mātānnapūrṇēśvarī//9//

O Mother Annapoorneshvari, please bestow alms upon me. The splendor of Your form is greater even than that of thousands of moons, suns and fires combined together. Your lips resemble rare and luscious fruit and are as pleasant as moonlight. In beauty You surpass the celestial orbs. In Your hands You clasp a garland, a book, a rope and a goad. Ruler of Kasipura, You are the embodiment of mercy.

Kṣatratrāṇakarī mahābhayakarī
mātā kṛpāsāgarī
sākṣānmōkṣakarī sadā śivakarī
viśvēśvaraśrīdharī
dakṣākrandakarī nirāmayakarī
kāśīpurādhīśvarī

bhikṣām dēhi kṛpāvalambanakarī mātānnapūrṇēśvarī//10//

O Mother Annapoorneshvari, please bestow alms upon me. You grant protection like a warrior and thus dispel all fears. O mother, ocean of kindness, You provide all with happiness. Auspicious one, You hold sway over this universe and control destiny. You brought great distress to Daksha Prajapati. All ailments are cured by You. Ruler of Kasipura, You are the embodiment of mercy.

Aṇṇapūrnē sadāpūrnē śaṅkaraprāṇavallabhē jñānavairāgya siddhyartham bhikṣām dēhi cha pārvati//11//

O Annapoorna, You are ever full. Radiating the essence of life, never exhausted, O partner of Shankara, grant to me that I become fully established in knowledge and renunciation.

Mātā mē pārvatī dēvi pitā dēvō mahēśvaraḥ bāndhavāḥ śivabhaktāścha svadēśō bhuvanatrayam//12//

Parvati Devi is my Divine Mother and Lord Mahesvara is my Father. My family encompasses the devotees of Shiva; all the three worlds are my native lands.

MAHIṢĀSURA MARDINĪ STŌTRAM

Ayi giri nandini nandita mēdini
viśva vinōdini nanda nutē
giri varavindya śirōdhi nivāsini
viṣṇu vilāsini jiṣṇunutē
bhagavati hē śitikaṇṭha kuṭumbini
bhūrikuṭumbini bhūrikṛtē
jaya jaya hē mahiṣāsura mardini
ramya kapardini śaila sutē/1/

Salutations, O Mother. You are a supreme delight to Your father (the Himalayas) as it is You who have created the whole universe as if in play. You are the happiness of all the beings in the creation. Your praises are sung even by Nandi (the vehicle of Shiva.) You reside on the lofty peaks of the Vindhya mountain range. Vishnu derives his creative power from You. Even the God Indra prays to none other than You. To You, the whole world is one family.

Sura vara varṣiṇi durdhara dharṣiṇi
durmukhamarṣiṇi harṣaratē
tribhuvana pōṣiṇi śaṅkara tōṣiṇi
kalmaṣa mōṣiṇi ghōṣaratē
danu jani rōṣiṇi ditisuta rōṣiṇi
durmada śōṣiṇi sindu sutē
jaya jaya hē mahiṣāsura mardini
ramya kapardini śaila sutē/2/

May victory be Yours, O Mother. You shower boons on the Gods. The giant Dhurdhara and the evil Durmukha were subdued by You. Established in imperishable bliss and delighting others, You sustain the three worlds. You are the bliss of the God Shiva. The war-cries of the asuras enraged You and You annihilated them. Of the evil-minded You are intolerant. To the egoistic Durmada You were the vehicle of death. You are the daughter of the ocean.

Ayi jagadamba madamba kadamba
vana priya vāsini hāsaratē
śikhari śirōmaṇi tuṅgahimālaya
śṛṅganijālaya madhyagatē
madhu madhurē madhukaiṭabha bhañjini
kaiṭabha bhañjini rāsaratē
jaya jaya hē mahiṣāsura mardini
ramya kapardini śaila sutē/3/

May victory be Yours, O Mother! You are my own Mother as well as the universal Mother of all of creation. The Kadamba forest is Your sacred dwelling place. You also abide on the majestic peaks of the Himalayan mountains. A pleasant smile, sweeter than honey, adorns Your beautiful face. The demons Madhu and Kaitabha were destroyed by You. You cleanse Your devotees of impurities and You rejoice in the divine rasa dance.

Ayi śata khaṇda vikhaṇḍita ruṇḍa
vituṇḍita śuṇḍa gajādhipatē
ripugaja gaṇḍa vidāraṇa chaṇḍa
parā krama śauṇḍa mṛgādhipatē
nija bhujadaṇḍa nipātitachaṇḍa
vipātita muṇḍa bhaṭādhipatē
jaya jaya hē mahiṣāsura mardini
ramya kapardini śaila sutē/4/

Glory to You, O Mother. With the weapon called Shatakhanda You beheaded Your demonic enemies and cut them into hundreds of pieces. Your vehicle, the lion, destroyed the immense elephants of Your enemies while You destroyed the armies of the asuras with deadly blows from Your powerful hands.

Ayi raṇa durmada śatru vadhōdita
durdhara nirjara śakti bhṛtē
chatura vichāra dhurīṇa mahā śiva
dūta kṛta pramathādhipatē
durita durīha durāśaya durmati
dānava dūta kṛtānta matē
jaya jaya hē mahiṣāsura mardini
ramya kapardini śaila sutē/5/

By annihilating the hordes of demons You reduced the heavy burden that had been carried by Mother Earth. You chose the introverted yogi, Shiva, as Your messenger to seek peace but, ultimately, You destroyed the insidious intentions of the asuras.

Ayi śaraṇāgata vairivadhūvara
vīravarābhaya dāyi karē
tribhu vana mastaka śūla virōdhi
śirōdhi kṛtāmala śūlakarē
dumi dumi tāmara dundubhināda
mahōmukharīkṛta diṅgikarē
jaya jaya hē mahiṣāsura mardini
ramya kapardini śaila sutē/6/

O Mother, You granted boons to the wives of the asuras who sought refuge in You. Yet You were merciless to the other demons who remained a menace to creation. You used Your trident to behead them. This act was praised by the Gods who played on their drums and thus filled all of creation with the rhythmic sound of their instruments.

Ayi nija huṅkṛti mātra nirākṛta
dhūmra vilōchana dhūmraśatē
sama ravi śōṣita śōṇita bīja
samut bhava śōṇita bījalatē
śiva śiva śumbha niśumbha mahāhava
tarpita bhūta piśāchapatē
jaya jaya hē mahiṣāsura mardini
ramya kapardini śaila sutē/7/

O Mother, as if through a miracle the syllable "hum," which You loudly uttered, reduced Dhumralochana and his evil allies to ashes. You destroyed Raktabija and his accomplices and You valiantly fought and killed Sumbha and Nisumbha. That act was pleasing to Shiva, the Lord of ghosts and ghouls.

Dhanu ranu ṣaṅga raṇakṣaṇa saṅga
parisphura daṅga naṭat kaṭakē
kanaka piśanga pṛṣatkaniṣaṅga
rasad bhaṭaśṛṅga hatā baṭukē
kṛta chatu raṅga balakṣiti raṅga
ghaṭad bahuraṅga raṭad baṭukē
jaya jaya hē mahiṣāsura mardini
ramya kapardini śaila sutē/8/

O Mother, while wielding weapons in battle the bangles on Your hands jingled rhythmically. The bells tied to Your waistband shined and blinded Your enemies. Huge birds of prey hovered over the slain bodies of Your enemies who were scattered on the battlefield.

Sura lalanā tatathō tatathō
tatathō bhinayōttara nṛtyaratē
kṛta kukuthahō kukuthō gaḍadādika
tāla kutūhala gānaratē
dhudhukuṭa dhukkuṭa dhim dhimita dhvani
dhīra mṛdaṅga ninādaratē
jaya jaya hē mahiṣāsura mardini
ramya kapardini śaila sutē/9/

O Mother, the source of sound, You rejoice at the movements of celestial dancers who dance to the rythym of the sounds "tatato-tatato-tatato" and "kukutha-kukutha-kukutha" and "ga-ga-dha." Their drum beats create the sounds "kuthu-dhukuta-dhimi."

Jaya jaya japya jayē jaya śabda
parastuti tatpara viśvanutē
jhaṇajhaṇa jhim jhimi jhiṅkṛta nūpura
śijñita mōhita bhūtapatē
naṭi tana ṭārdha naṭīnaṭanāyaka
nāṭitanāṭya sugānaratē
jaya jaya hē mahiṣāsura mardini
ramya kapardini śaila sutē/10/

O Mother, all of the devotees sing to You, "Victory! Victory!" You dance in union with Shiva during His Tandava dance and He becomes pleased with the jingling sound that emanates from Your anklets.

Ayi sumanaḥ sumanaḥ sumanaḥ
sumanaḥ sumanōhara kāntiyutē
śritarajanī rajanī rajanī rajanī
rajanīkara vaktra yutē
sunayana vibhramara bhramara
bhramara bhramara bhramarādhipatē
jaya jaya hē mahiṣāsura mardini
ramya kapardini śaila sutē/11/

O Mother, the Devas mentally offer You worship with flowers and Your beauty assumes the form of the flower blossoms that the Devas visualize. Your face resembles a lotus that floats in a lake illuminated by the moon. The curls of Your hair toss like bees and add beauty to Your eyes.

Mahita mahāhava mallamatallika
vallita rallaka bhalliratē
vira chita vallika pallika mallika
jhillika bhillika vargavṛtē
sita kṛta phulla samulla sitāruṇa
tallaja pallava sallalitē
jaya jaya hē mahiṣāsura mardini
ramya kapardini śaila sutē/12/

O Mother, when warriors unleash their weapons on a field of battle it is You who watches over them. You are the refuge even to the hilldwellers and the tribal people that live in creepers and vines. When the twelve Adityas wait upon and serve You then You shine even more brilliantly.

Aviralla gaṇḍa galanmada mēdura
matta mataṅgaja rājapatē
tribhuvana bhūṣaṇa bhūta kalānidhi
rūpa payōnidhi rāja sutē
ayi sudatījana lālasa mānasa
mōhana manmatha rājasutē
jaya jaya hē mahiṣāsura mardini
ramya kapardini śaila sutē/13/

O Mother, Your majestic walk is like that of the king of the elephants from whose temple riches flow abundantly. You arose from the ocean as Maha Lakshmi along with the moon that adorns the three worlds. Manmatha, who infatuates young damsels, holds You in awe as he is powerless to enslave You with desire.

Kamala dalāmala kōmala kānti
kalākalitāmala bhālalatē
sakalavilāsa kalānilaya krama
kēli chalat kalahamsa kulē
alikula saṅkula kuvalaya maṇḍala
maulimilad bakulālikulē
jaya jaya hē mahiṣāsura mardini
ramya kapardini śaila sutē/14/

O Mother, Your beautiful forehead, which is broad and without match, excels even the lotus petals in luster. Your graceful movements are like that of the beautiful swan. The bakula flowers that lovingly adorn Your flowing hair attract swarms of bees.

Karamulīrava vījitakūjita
lajjita kōkila mañjumatē
milita pulinda manōhara guñjita
rañjita śaila nikuñjagatē
nijaguṇa bhūta mahāśabarīgaṇa
sad guṇa sambhṛta kēliratē
jaya jaya hē mahiṣāsura mardini
ramya kapardini śaila sutē/15/

O Mother, the melodious notes emanating from Your flute cause the cuckoo to cease his song. In the Kalisha garden, You stand to watch the hunter women, Your devoted followers, and the bees hum sweetly.

Kaṭitaṭa pītadukūla vichitra
mayūkha tiras kṛta chandraruchē
praṇata surāsura mauli maṇisphura
damśu lasannakha chandra ruchē
jita kanakāchala mauli madōrjjita
nirbhara kuñjara kumbhakuchē
jaya jaya hē mahiṣāsura mardini
ramya kapardini śaila sutē//16//

O Mother, the shining garment that You wear on Your slim waist excels the splendor of the moon. The nails on Your toes glow brightly and their radiance is enhanced greatly by the crowns of both the suras and the asuras who prostrate in reverence before You. Your breasts are like the peaks of the Himalayas covered by waterfalls.

Vijita sahasra karaika sahasra
karaika sahasra karaika nutē
kṛta suratāraka saṅgaratāraka
saṅgaratāraka sūnusutē
suratha samādhi samāna samādhi
samādhi samādhi sujātaratē
jaya jaya hē mahiṣāsura mardini
ramya kapardini śaila sutē//17//

O Mother, the luster of the sun fades before You and the sun surrenders to You by pouring thousands of his rays at Your divine feet. The son of Tarakasura praises You profusely after the war. You delight to manifest in the mantra that is chanted with devotion by such devotees as Suratha and Samadhi in Saptasati.

Padakamalam karunānilayē
vari vasyati yōnudinam nuśivē
ayi kamalē kamalānilayē
kamalānilayaḥ sa katham na bhavēt
tava padamēva param padamitya
nuśīlayatō mama kim na śivē
jaya jaya hē mahiṣāsura mardini
ramya kapardini śaila sutē//18//

O Mother, Parvati, worship that is performed for You grants one prosperity as You are also Maha Lakshmi Herself. Worshiping and meditating upon Your sacred feet will bring one to the final state of liberation.

Kanakalasat kala sindhujalai
ranuṣiñchati tē guṇa raṅga bhuvam
bhajati sa kim na śachīkuchakumbha
taṭīparirambha sukhānu bhavam
tava charaṇam śaraṇam karavāṇi

mṛḍhāni sadāmayi dēhi śivam
jaya jaya hē mahiṣāsura mardini
ramya kapardini śaila sutē//19//

O Mother, even a sweeper in Your courtyard inherits all heavenly pleasures. Be pleased to accept my humble service and grant to me whatever You consider to be good for me.

Tava vimalēndukulam vadanēndu
malam sakalam nanukūlayatē
kimu puruhūtapurīndumukhī
sumukhībirasau vimukhīkriyatē
mama tu matam śivanāmadhanē
bhavatī kṛpayā kimuta kriyatē
jaya jaya hē mahiṣāsura mardini
ramya kapardini śaila sutē//20//

O Mother, none of the celestial beauties can even tempt one who meditates upon Your beautiful face. O Mother of Shiva's heart, please fulfill my life.

Ayi mayi dīnadayālutayā
kṛpayaiva tvayā bhavitavyamumē
ayi jagatō jananī kṛpayāsi
yathāsi tathānimitāsi ramē
yaduchita matra bhavatyurarī
kurutāduru tāpamapākuru mē
jaya jaya hē mahiṣāsura mardini
ramya kapardini śaila sutē//21//

O Mother, Are You not renowned for Your compassion? Be merciful to me, my Mother. Please grant to me the removal of all of my sorrows.

English songs

DEEP WITHIN THE SOUL

**Deep within the soul of everyone,
hidden in most everything under the sun,
is a place we call our home
where differences don't belong.**

**Visions of the Rishis gave us sight,
showing us how peace can reign in every life,
to become a ray of light
for those who live in endless night.**

**Ignorance has always lead to war,
indifference has warned us
countless times before.
Intellect can do no more
in the quest to reach our goal.**

**Close your eyes forget the names and forms,
concentrate on God or love and go beyond.
Truth alone can be your home
a place that you can call your own.**

EVERYWHERE I LOOK

**Everywhere I look I find You,
all that I hear is the sound of You,
only one name on my breath,
Krishna, Krishna, O my Krishna.**

**What have I done, O my dear Krishna,
that has caused You to go away?
My eyes cry for a glimpse of You, Krishna.
When will You come, Krishna,
when will You come?**

**Though You have left me, my dear Krishna,
You can never ever leave my mind.
You are inside of me, Krishna,
in each and every beat of my heart.**

GIVE ME DEVOTION

**Give me devotion,
Give me pure love, Amma,
Give me firm faith in You,
Protect me, O Amma.**

GIVE US YOUR GRACE

**Give us Your Grace, O my Lord,
that this mind will never wander.
May it always chant the song of selflessness
and speak the language of love.**

**When this life brings happiness and joy
may I never forget You.
And in times of sorrow and sadness
let me always have faith in You.**

When my time comes to leave Earth
may I find You beside me.
May my lips ever chant Your name, Lord,
let my mind ever dwell in You.

GRACE US WITH YOUR COMPASSION

Grace us with Your compassion Lord,
I have no one but You my Lord.

You create this world by Your whim,
You destroy this world by Your will.
You turn our sorrows into joy,
I have no one but You my Lord.

You are my friend and my family,
mother and father my everything.
You are my sole refuge O Lord,
I have no one but You my Lord.

O Lord I don't know anything,
only Your glories I know to sing.
If I were to leave where would I go,
I have no one but You my Lord.

LIFE IS A PLAY

Life is a play so enchanting.
All this world is divinely created.
No end or beginning to this mystery,
Mother, Your play is eternal.

**Millions of forms are born out of unity,
creating the universe we see.
Mother, Your smile becomes our creation
blossoming garden eternal.**

**Long, long ago in a heavenly dream,
Your dream was a vast golden sea.
We were the waves always rising and falling,
how can we tell Your story?**

**What is the purpose of praising and blaming,
taking the play to be real?
We are the actors in Your divine play,
how can we sing Your glories?**

LORD OF VRINDAVAN

**O Lord of Vrindavan,
give me Your darshan.
Shower Your Grace upon
this lonely one.**

**When will You come, Krishna,
when will You come?**

**Let the beauty of my Lord
ever fill this heart with love,
everywhere and evermore,
Bhagavan Krishna.**

**Let the glory of Your play
never leave these lips again.
Ever sing the holy name, Bhagavan Krishna.**

Let me cry and pray and call
for a life of serving all.
Everything I do is for
Bhagavan Krishna

Let me feel You all the time,
let my heart become Your shrine,
never leave this child behind
Bhagavan Krishna.

MOTHER BLESS ME

Mother bless me with a vision
of Your form divine.
Only by Your grace can I
swim from darkness to light.

Mother bless me with devotion,
bless me with pure love.
Bless me with eternal faith,
protect me, O Mother.

Without Your sweet form beside me
life would have no meaning.
What my heart is longing for
is to merge in You.

You are the essence of my life,
You are my true love.
Always let me love and serve
is all I ask of You.

Just a single glimpse of You
thrills me to the core.
Never let me stray afar
keep me close to You.

MOTHER YOUR WILL

Mother, Your will is the source of the universe.
All that occurs is Your divine play.

We think our actions are in our control.
You are the power behind all we do.

You are the one who creates and destroys,
She who forms Maya then takes it away.

Only with grace can we carry these sorrows,
filled with Your love we abandon all fear.

Mother, You give us the fruits of our actions,
they may be sweet or bitter and hard.

I am the carriage, You hold the reins,
I am the house, Amma, You dwell within.

Mother, I pray to surrender my life to You,
laying my will at Your holy feet.

ONE TINY ATOM

One tiny atom helpless I float
in this infinite universe.
Come to me, my dearest Lord,
comfort me today.

Promise to come right away,
promise to take my sorrows away.
You are the ruler of all of the worlds,
please come and help me today.

Give me thoughts of virtue and bliss,
teach me the way of kindness and peace.
Help me to always love and serve,
You who are my Lord.

I always want to be chanting Your name
hoping You'll come before me I pray.
Closing my eyes I see You inside,
O Lord, You are my own.

WHERE CAN I GO?

If this is not a place where
tears are understood,
where can I go,
where can I go to cry?

If this is not a place where
my spirit can take wing,
where can I go,
where can I go to fly?

If this is not a place where
my questions can be asked
where can I go,
where can I go to seek?

If this is not a place where
my feelings can be heard
where can I go,
where can I go to speak?

If this is not a place You'll
accept me as I am
where can I go,
where can I go to be?

Where can I learn and grow?
Where can I just be me?
Amma, where can I just be me?

WONDROUS GODDESS PRECIOUS GODDESS

Wondrous Goddess precious Goddess
giver of the gift of grace,
lighting fires of liberation
please remove my many sorrows.

With its pleasures and its troubles
I have seen this worldly life.
Must I suffer like the moth who
blindly flies into the fire?

I am pleading for Thy grace to
hold me firmly on the path.
Mother who destroys all sadness
please remove my many sorrows.

What the eyes can see today
by tomorrow will not ever stay.
Clouded by the veil of maya
only what is true remains.

Asking You with humility
to know the fruit of human birth.
Merciful and radiant Goddess
lovingly I bow to Thee.

YOU ARE CREATION

You are creation,
You are creator,
You are the source of life,
You are eternal truth.

You have created
all of this universe.
You are the beginning,
You are the ending.

You are the Essence
of all that we see.
You are the soul within
and all of nature.

Index of Bhajans Volume 5

www.ingramcontent.com/pod-product-compliance
Lightning Source LLC
LaVergne TN
LVHW051551080426
835510LV00020B/2954